THE MIND OF YOUR DOG

UNDERSTANDING THE PSYCHE AND INTELLECT OF MANS' BEST FRIEND

JAMES AUSTIN VANDERBILT

J.A.V

*To my love and soul partner in life J. L. M., to my family and friends, I appreciate all of the support you've shown me on this amazing journey, **thank you** from the bottom of my heart*

Jupiter Thunder, you're such an amazing and awesome pup - I love you forever!

indirect, that are incurred as a result of the use of the information contained within this document, including, but not limited to, errors, omissions, or inaccuracies.

CONTENTS

Introduction   xv

1. A BRIEF HISTORY OF DOGS AND US   1
   Domestication   2
   Symbiosis   6
   Dogs With a Job   9
   Companion Dogs   10

2. THE FIVE SENSES   12
   Smell   14
   Sight   18
   Hearing   21
   Touch   23
   Taste   26
   Living in a Dog's World   27

3. A DOG'S CHARACTERISTICS AND   31
   PERSONALITIES
   Emotion   34
   Temperament   41
   Age   43
   Environment Matters   47

4. TYPES OF DOG   51
   Dog Breeds   53
   Matching Dogs to Families   68

5. HOW A DOG LEARNS   76
   Social Learning and Observation   80
   Association (Classical Conditioning)   82
   Operant Conditioning   83

6. ENCOURAGING GOOD BEHAVIOR   86
Problem Behaviors   90
Spend Time Together   97
It Won't Be Cute When They're Grown Up   99

7. UNDERSTANDING WHAT YOUR DOG SAYS TO YOU   100
Five Types of Communication   101
Body Language   105
Vocalization   116
Talking Just to You   123

8. HOW TO TALK TO YOUR DOG   127
The Pack Mentality   131
Socialization   137
Working With a Puppy   138
Basic Commands for Everyday Life   140
Formal Obedience Training   151
Canine Sports and Activities   155
Specialty Training   159

Living the Best Life With Your Dog   163
References   169
Images   187

Welcome to the JRT Tribe!

Join our community of puppy and dog owners just like you in my Facebook group:

House of The Jack Russell Terrier

(https://www.facebook.com/groups/houseofthejackrussellterrier)

We've made it easy to join the Facebook Group, scan the QR-code below:

A dog's mind is incredibly precious... all they desire is your love, a cozy bed, food and some playtime. But most of all, to be around you, that's the highlight of their day

INTRODUCTION

I have had a life-long love of dogs.

I was born in New York City and we did not have a dog in the city, but I moved to the Bay Area of Northern California when I was three years old.

I always loved animals, especially puppies. So you can imagine my delight when I was six, and I got home from school one day to find a tiny puppy sitting on the living room floor! The puppy, quickly named Jack, was a Jack Russell Terrier.

Hi There

Jack and I were quite a pair. We had a lot of fun.

A couple of years later, I wanted to teach him some tricks. I was only eight, so I could not do it alone. But I helped train Jack, and I have been helping family and friends to train their dogs ever since.

If you know anything about Jack Russell Terriers, you know they can be little terrors. They are tiny, but they are bouncing balls of energy. And they know that they are the boss of the world! Jack was no exception.

What could be better for an eight-year-old boy? Jack and I did everything together. We ran through the house and yard, bounced on the bed, climbed up and down the sliding board, and even played soccer (Jack loved to steal the ball and he could dribble like no one's business).

Luckily, my parents are both very calm and decisive people. They made sure Jack knew who was boss and they helped me learn how to handle him. Jack always let us know what he wanted, but he also understood and listened when we said "No."

I know from personal experience how important it is to train a dog in order for the dog to get along with her human 'pack.' Puppies and dogs—and their owners—need to have the proper training to give them the tools to be able to live together happily.

Jack lived with me for seven wonderful years. I have had other great dogs: Chihuahua, Doberman, Chow Chow, Rottweiler, and Miniature Pinscher. But the Jack Russell Terrier has a special place in my heart.

After a lifetime spent with dogs, I know that in order to raise a happy, successful companion dog, it is important to understand things from the dog's point of view. I am passionate about helping people understand their dogs' needs and then helping them use that knowledge, combined with positive reinforcement and love, to create a happy, friendly and loveable family dog.

Dogs—these beautiful creatures—are always there for us, rain or shine, always providing silly, laughable, and lovable moments.

I have another Jack Russell Terrier now. This Jack Russell, Max, is 10 years old. He is a wonderful buddy to always have around. He goes with us into the mountains to enjoy the snow or into the city. He goes on camping trips, to birthday parties, and even to casinos. He is a great companion on long trips. In fact, we almost took him to Hawaii last year, but I did not think he'd enjoy the plane ride!

Today I have an excellent idea about what Max wants and what he may be thinking. But there were many times when Max was a pup that I wondered if I was meeting his needs—according to him.

Max has never talked to me in words, but after all the time we have spent together in the last 10 years, I know now what he typically wants or what he is thinking. Some of this is Max-specific. But a large part is based on the fact that I understand when Max is talking dog.

What a dog needs and how a dog communicates is based on the fact that he is a dog. Understanding that is the important first step toward creating a healthy, happy bond.

This book is my attempt to share what I have learned with you. It is not hard; it simply takes considering things from your dog's point of view.

You can easily use the information in this book to strengthen the communication between you and your dog.

A BRIEF HISTORY OF DOGS AND US

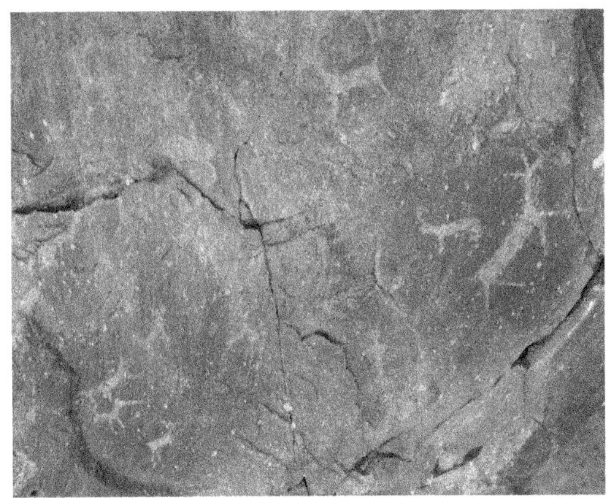

Dogs and humans have been living together for many thousands of years. Over the centuries, we have learned to know each other and how to get along.

At first the relationship was simple. We can not know for sure, but it seems likely that the wolf, ancestor of the dog, discovered that one easy way to get food was to scavenge scraps left by humans. Over time some of these animals got comfortable being close to the humans. Perhaps especially friendly dogs even cuddled up to share the warmth on very cold nights.

As time went by the relationship grew. Humans started to learn about dogs' special abilities. They bred dogs to enhance different abilities, creating partners who could help them to hunt, raise livestock, and do many other jobs.

In our modern world, we do not have the same relationship with dogs as in the past. Urbanization and industrialization have changed the world we share. Most of us no longer ask our dogs to do much work. They are simply companions.

But none of this has changed the fundamental character of the dog, or the dynamic between humans and dogs.

DOMESTICATION

The domestication and breeding of dogs is part of human history. From the beginning people selected and bred dogs to encourage traits they liked.

There is even a theory that it was the relationship between humans and dogs that explains why early, nomadic humans thrived while Neanderthals declined (Garber, 2012). The theory goes that the early dogs helped humans in three ways. They helped find prey. They helped with hauling: bringing back game from the hunt and moving camp from place to place. And in hunting, dogs may even have given humans an advantage due to the fact that the whites of human eyes reveal where we are looking. Dogs' eyes do not do this. So once prey was sighted, the early humans may have been able to give eye signals to their dogs, and the dogs could respond by flushing the prey.

Dogs were the first animals to be domesticated. This happened because dogs and humans could help each other, not because humans wanted to raise dogs for food. Dogs have evolved to cooperate with human beings in a kind of mutual benefit society.

There is some genetic evidence that suggests this may have happened because the wolf that became the domestic dog had a genetic mutation for hyper-sociability. We will never know. But it is certainly possible that hyper-social wolves and fearless young humans started the process that led to the modern dog.

Modern dogs and wolves descended from a common ancestor, a now-extinct type of wolf, at a time when human beings were hunter gatherers. We know this because even today the genetic relationship between dogs and wolves is so close that gray wolves and dogs have nearly identical DNA. They are capable of mating and producing fertile offspring.

The earliest fossil evidence of domesticated dogs comes from remains found in a 14,000-year-old grave in Oberkassel, which is just outside of Bonn in western Germany. The grave contained a couple and a young puppy. By examining the bones, scientists learned that the puppy had been sickly and had been cared for over a long period of time (Katz, 2018).

Another grave, this one from 6,000 years ago, was found in Saudi Arabia that contained the remains of six adults, an adolescent, four children, and an arthritic dog, suggesting a close relationship between the dog and humans (Baker, 2021).

Other evidence for the relationship between dogs and humans is seen in art. There are pictures of dogs on 8,000-year-old pottery from Iran. Prehistoric cave paintings in the Arabian Peninsula from around the same time show dogs being used in hunts. In the paintings it even looks like some of the dogs are on leashes.

The evidence suggests that the dog-human relationship was not simply utilitarian. Yes, dogs were used for hunting, but it seems that they were also being cared for as pets.

We can not be sure when dogs were domesticated. Estimates range from 10,000 to 33,000 years ago. But we do know that there are certain physical characteristics found in most domesticated animals. These include a tendency to have spots on their fur, and to have floppy ears, smaller heads, shorter tails, and big eyes. All of which is to say that, in general, domestic animals tend to resemble the younger versions of their wild cousins, maintaining an almost baby-like appearance.

There is a famous Russian experiment that sheds some light on how this process of domestication might have happened.

The experiment started in 1959 and continues today. The scientists worked with silver foxes, which are closely related to wolves. Within forty years, they created a new type of fox, a domestic fox with different genes than the wild foxes.

How did it work? The foxes were bred in two lines: one for tameness and one for aggression toward humans. Breeding decisions were made only on the basis of tameness or aggression. Physical characteristics were not considered. Foxes that would accept food from the hands of a human were mated. The others were not.

Over the course of generations, the tame foxes developed similar physical characteristics to the modern dog: floppy ears, curly tails, and shorter snouts. The tame foxes wag their tails when they are happy, and they like to be with humans (Goldman, 2010).

Archeologists have found fossil remains to show that, by the end of the stone age and beginning of the Bronze age, there were five different types of domestic dog: wolf-type dogs and mastiffs (guard dogs), pointers and sight hounds (hunting dogs), and herding dogs. Each had been bred to work with people in a particular way (Vanacore, 2019).

SYMBIOSIS

In the process of domestication, dogs and humans have developed a mutually beneficial relationship.

Dogs have evolved to get along with humans. They can read our tone of voice and our gestures. They respond to our emotions.

There was a study done at the University of Lincoln in Great Britain that shows how dogs read us. We know that humans have what is called a left gaze bias. This means that when we look at someone, we scan their face from left to right to focus on the right side, which is better at expressing emotions. Dogs have learned to do this too, but only with people. They do not do it with other dogs (Stilwell, 2016).

Dogs also respond to human gestures. A dog will pay attention when we point to something. This is something that neither the dog's nearest relative (a wolf) nor the human's nearest relative (a chimpanzee) can do (Viegas, 2012).

In addition to emotion and gestures, dogs understand human language. When we speak to them, they understand at least some of the words we say. There are even some dogs that show a remarkable ability to understand what people say.

You may have heard of two amazing dogs, Chaser and Stella. These dogs are examples of the dog's potential facility with human language.

Chaser was a Border Collie who became known as the smartest dog in the world. Her owner was Jack Pilley, a professor of psychology. Dr. Pilley realized that dogs could understand language when he learned about farmers who trained their dogs to cull specific sheep from a herd by using a command like, "Get Tillie," and he wondered how much human language his dog could learn.

Over 15 years, Dr. Pilley taught Chaser more than 1,000 proper nouns. Chaser learned the difference between these words and commands about them. She knew how to find and retrieve specific, named objects. She could even select an object she'd never seen before when she was asked to pick it out of a group of things she already knew.

Another dog, Stella, is showing that dogs can actually use human language.

Stella is a Blue Heeler/Catahoula mix whose human is Christina Hunger, a speech therapist. Hunger teaches pre-linguistic toddlers, and she wondered if she could teach Stella to talk by using a device similar to the one she uses with her non-verbal human patients. So she built a board with a couple of buttons, each of which could be pushed to play a word.

It worked. In three years, Stella learned more than 45 words and then started to put the words together into phrases. She says things like "Come outside." She even learned to use words about how she was feeling. For example, one time she pushed the button to say "Mad" when she did not get a treat at the regular time.

Chaser and Stella are both highly trained examples of what dogs are capable of in terms of understanding human language. But as anyone who has ever lived with a dog knows, every dog 'talks.'

DOGS WITH A JOB

Just like people need a purpose, dogs need something to do. They need work.

In the wild, it is simple. A dog's job is to hunt for food. Living in the human world, the dog's job depends on his or her person.

Historically people have used dogs for jobs like tracking, retrieving, herding, pulling, running, and guarding. All of these jobs rely on dogs' abilities to use senses that are more powerful or acute than ours.

Many of the jobs that dogs do depend on their incredible sense of smell. From the beginning, hunting dogs used their sense of smell to find game, and herding dogs to find wandering sheep. In the Alps, dogs were used to find people buried under the snow.

Today, dogs sniff out all kinds of things. Military dogs sniff out landmines. Medical alert dogs can detect cancer and help control diabetes. Search and rescue dogs find lost children and help first responders during disasters. And dogs are helping us deal with environmental issues by doing things like detecting contaminated water, finding rare wild animals, and detecting invasive weeds.

We also have service dogs that are trained as guide dogs for the blind, mobility assistance dogs for the disabled, and assistance dogs for people with hearing loss.

COMPANION DOGS

Most dogs today are not working dogs. They are companions, pets. We do not expect our pets to do any specific job.

Companion dogs are not new. There is evidence from 3,000 years ago of small 'sleeve dogs' (today's Pekingese). Sleeve dogs were bred as pets for Chinese royalty. Evidence has also been found of other small pet dogs from several thousand years ago in the Americas and Europe (History of Companion Dogs, JaneDogs, n.d.).

Just as some dog breeds were developed to create working dogs, other breeds were developed to create companion pets. These were tiny dogs such as the Shih Tzu, Chihuahua, Maltese, and Cavalier King Charles Spaniel.

Dogs that are bred to be companion pets have a different disposition than working breeds. They are content to spend a lot of time relaxing and simply being together with their humans.

Today, however, people keep all types of dogs as companion pets. This can cause problems when the pet becomes destructive because she is bored simply hanging around the house. Perhaps it would be good for us and our dogs if we thought about being a companion as a kind of work.

I will talk some more about this as we go on. But first I would like to take a closer look at the distinct capabilities of the dog.

2

THE FIVE SENSES

Dogs and humans are both mammals. But the world looks very different to us both.

This is because the specifics of biology and brain structure for a dog are similar, but not the same, as for a human. For example, we both have four limbs. But dogs have paws and walk on all fours. We humans walk on two legs with feet; our other two limbs are arms with hands and opposable thumbs.

There are also some differences between a dog's brain and ours. Looking at all mammals, the dog's brain is 1.2 times larger than an average mammal brain compared to body weight. A human's brain is about 7 times larger.

However, the ratio of brain size compared to body weight does not always align with intelligence. The bigger difference between a dog and human brain lies in the composition of our brains. In humans, the frontal lobe represents about 30% of brain weight, compared to 10% for a dog (Berns, 2020).

The frontal lobe is the part of the brain that controls such higher-level executive functions as language, planning, judgment, and self-control. This is one of the reasons that it is so misleading to anthropomorphize what we see in our dogs.

However, dogs and humans do have the same five senses.

SMELL

Dogs see the world through their nose. Just how I wrote this sentence says a lot about a major difference between dogs and us. I used the word 'see,' which shows how humans experience the world mostly through eyesight, while dogs experience it through smell.

One of the problems of anthropomorphizing your dog is that it can dim your appreciation of this important difference between you and your dog. It might make you forget that a dog doesn't 'see' the world, so much as 'smell' it.

We have all experienced the way that smells can trigger memory and emotion. Some people, like wine tasters or perfumers, train themselves to recognize a great many smells. In fact, humans can actually smell quite a lot.

We know this from Helen Keller, who could neither see nor hear, and so relied on smell and touch to perceive the world around her. Helen Keller could smell when a storm was coming. She could tell whether a person was a carpenter, ironworker, artist, mason, or chemist by how they smelled.

But people who can see and hear do not have nearly as fine an awareness of the world of smell as does a dog. We can develop our sense of smell, but we perceive the world first through our eyes.

Dogs perceive the world first through their nose. Each individual person has a unique scent signature, and your smell is how your dog recognizes you. While this may not sound great at first blush, we love that they do not care what we look like!

Humans have a dim perception of this when they experience a loved one as having an appealing scent.

Smell is your dog's dominant sense. Scent hounds have a particularly powerful sense of smell, but in general dogs have a sense of smell that is anywhere from 10,000 to 100,000 times more powerful than a human's.

We do not really know how powerful a dog's nose is because we do not have instruments that can measure the limits of the dogs' ability. But we know that, while a dog's brain is about 1/10th the size of a human's, their olfactory cortex (which processes smell) is 40 times larger.

Dogs have 250 million scent receptors compared to our five million. They are able to detect odors in parts per trillion. A dog can be trained to identify the scent of banana diluted to one or two parts per trillion, or detect TNT at one trillionth of a gram (Horowitz, 2016).

A dog's nose also has something a human's does not: a vomeronasal organ, also called Jacobsen's organ. Jacobsen's organ is a secondary olfactory system that connects directly to the brain and is designed to detect moisture rather than air-borne particles. This is why dogs have moist noses.

In addition to simply having more scent receptors, dogs can use each nostril separately. This lets them gather scents from all directions. They also have two nasal passages, so they can breathe air in and out at the same time.

This means that, unlike humans who smell and breathe through the same passage, scenting and breathing are separate functions for a dog. A person might take a deep breath to smell something, but when we exhale, we push the odor molecules back out. When a dog inhales a scent, it goes through their olfactory system independently of taking the next breath.

We often talk about dogs 'marking their territory,' probably because when we take our dogs for a walk they pee everywhere. However, domestic dogs do not pee to mark their territory, they do this to leave a message. Canine researcher Alexandra Horowitz calls it "graffiti" (Horowitz, 2016).

What kind of information does all this urine contain? It carries the chemical signature of all kinds of things: sex, age, health, recent meals, the environment, time, and emotion. "Time?" You say. Yes, odor fades over time. A stronger smell is more recent. And because odor is carried to us in the air, your dog can smell something that is on the way.

Dogs like to take their time to smell the world.

I saw a great cartoon about this in *The New Yorker*. A woman is standing on a city street with her dog on a leash. The dog is reclining under a tree, reading a book with a cup of coffee nearby, and the woman is saying, "Take your time." (Cartoons from the November 15, 2021 Issue, 2021).

When you think about what Helen Keller was able to perceive using her sense of smell, imagine what smells tell your dog! This is why dogs sniff so much on a walk. They are learning a lot.

What does scent tell your dog about you? Your dog can smell how you feel. This is because certain glands are activated by our emotions. So the ability for dogs to smell emotions like fear is real. In fact, everything we do—running, hugging a friend, playing tennis, sitting in an office or classroom—carries a chemical signal that creates a recognizable scent.

SIGHT

Dogs are born with their eyes closed. They do not begin to see until they are two weeks old.

Where seeing is our primary way of approaching the world, a dog's sight is more limited. Your dog can visually perceive the same things you do. But like most mammals, dogs have tw0-color vision. They see black and white and shades of yellowish green and blue violet. They do not see red and green, and they can not see the difference in hue between red, orange, and yellow.

Because a dog's eyes are on the side of their head instead of in front like ours, however, dogs do have a wider field of view. A dog's visual field extends about 240 degrees compared to our 180 degrees.

Dogs also see movement more clearly than they see the details of objects. Good motion perception was a benefit in the wild, helping dogs find prey relatively well at all hours, and especially at the critical hunting times of dawn and dusk.

On the other hand, dogs do not have as accurate close-up vision as we do. Because of the position of their eyes, when they are looking at things up close they see better to the sides than straight ahead. Most can not focus clearly on objects that are a foot away. But their powerful sense of smell makes up the difference.

Dogs with longer muzzles tend to have better side-to-side vision; these are the dogs that love to play ball. Dogs with flatter faces can not follow the ball as well and probably do not enjoy chasing it.

A dog's eyes have another feature that is not part of the human eye. This is a thin membrane behind the retina called the tapetum that reflects light from an object back through the eye a second time. The effect of the tapetum is to nearly double your dog's ability to see in low light.

Have you ever noticed your dog's eyes gelam in the beam of a flashlight or when his eyes reflect a car's headlights? That is the tapetum, reflecting light back to you.

And one other advantage the dog has is related to how a mammal's eyes perceive motion.

When we see something move, we do not see it as a steady stream. Instead, our eyes are sending a sequence of images, one after the other, to our brain. In this, human vision works very much like film or video. In the movies, it is called 'frame rate.'

Dogs and people both see motion this way. But, where humans perceive about 60 images every second, dogs perceive 70 or 80. The impact of this can be compared to slow motion in a movie. Slow motion is created by recording more frames per second, with the result that slow motion lets you see each movement more clearly. So the dog's slightly higher visual frame rate gives them a little more visual acuity.

Sight is also important to a dog because so much of how a dog communicates is through body language. Yes, dogs can vocalize, but they do not use words (only humans do that). Much of what dogs say is communicated in body language. I will talk more about this in Chapter 7.

But in all, the differences between our vision and a dog's vision are subtle enough that we rarely need to consider them when we are communicating with our dogs. The biggest consideration is that your dog can pick up on very slight movement from you.

HEARING

Dogs can not hear when they are born but develop powerful hearing by the time they're a month old.

Dogs' ears are about four times more sensitive than ours. They can pick up sounds from all directions. And they can hear a much greater range of frequencies than we do. Humans and dogs have about the same low-range hearing, but dogs hear much higher pitched sounds. Humans can hear tones up t0 20,000 hertz. Dogs can hear up to 45,000 hertz.

Dogs also have longer ear canals than we do, with 18 muscles in each ear—three times more than we have. This lets them identify the source of a sound with great accuracy just by using their ears (we have to turn our heads and walk around to get the same information).

The result is that dogs hear much more than we do. They not only hear sounds we cannot perceive, they are also aware of sounds we routinely tune out.

It is easy to ignore how much a dog can hear when we are blind to things that are obvious to them.

One example of this that I have noticed with my dog is how he reacts to the sound of a dog barking on TV. Sometimes he barks back and sometimes he just ignores it. I think his response is actually because of the quality of the sound on those TV shows. He barks when the TV barking sounds real to him.

Many things in our world make sounds that we cannot hear, but our dogs can. Computers, electronic equipment, and household appliances all make high-pitched sounds that we simply do not hear. We do not hear the bugs that live inside our walls (thank goodness!). Most sounds from two blocks away are imperceptible to us.

One of the ways that we need to be considerate of our dogs is by being aware of sounds that may bother, or even hurt, them. For example, very noisy environments can damage your dog's hearing sooner than it will yours.

As you know, some dogs are very sensitive to certain sounds like a vacuum cleaner, garbage truck, thunderstorm, or Fourth of July fireworks. Sometimes their sensitivity causes extreme anxiety, and a recent study in Great Britain and Brazil has shown that this response can be because the dog is actually in pain (McReynolds, 2018).

As dog owners, we want to be aware of our dog's sound sensitivity, because it can be dangerous. I knew a Golden Retriever, Margo, who was so stressed by loud noises she would always hide or try to run away from them. One Fourth of July, while Margo's owner was away at a party, there were loud fireworks. Margo was so stressed she jumped out of a second story window trying to run away from the sound. Luckily, Margo was okay, but she could have been very badly hurt.

Desensitization is the typical remedy recommended for dogs with sound sensitivity, but if the problem is severe you may want to consult your vet to see if pain is involved. If loud noises are hurting your dog, there are remedies to provide relief.

TOUCH

Isn't it wonderful to pet and cuddle with your dog?

Like us, dogs enjoy a loving touch. My Jack Russell, Max, likes a vigorous rub on his sides and a nice long scratch down his spine. My Chow Chow, Rufus, on the other hand, had a deep, thick, furry coat and he loved me to dig my fingers in and rub vigorously. My Rottweiler loved a good tummy rub.

Except for the fact that they have whiskers and we have hands, a dog's sense of touch is very much like ours. Like us, they have receptors on their skin to feel pain, pressure, temperature, movement, and body position.

Since dogs are blind and deaf at birth, touch is one of a dog's first experiences. Remember, dogs do not have good close-up vision so the mother dog does not see her puppies as clearly as a person can. When her puppies are born, a mother dog uses touch to examine the puppies all over. The mother dog licks and nuzzles the puppies to comfort them, stimulate them to pee and poop, and keep them clean.

As the puppies grow and play with their littermates, they also learn the limits of touch. While they are chasing and tumbling together, they use their teeth and paws in play fights and learn to moderate their biting so they do not hurt each other. This is one big reason you should leave puppies with their mother and littermates until they are at least seven or eight weeks old.

Much like humans, dogs prefer to be touched by someone they know and trust. And like us, dogs are more and less sensitive in different places.

A dog's whiskers are very sensitive; they do not like to be touched there. This may be one reason dogs do not like it when a stranger greets them by reaching toward their face.

Some dogs have especially sensitive paws; they do not like to have their nails clipped. Others have very sensitive ears and do not like to have their ears cleaned.

Dogs like to touch their humans, too. Your dog will lean up against you, lick you, or snuggle up with you on the sofa (if you let your dog on the sofa).

Touch helps us form emotional bonds with each other and it has the power to make us feel good. Research even shows that petting a dog is good for you—and your dog,

Petting increases the levels of the oxytocin in the blood. This is the same hormone that is released, during sex, during other pleasurable skin contact like massage or a loving touch, or during other tender moments like when a mother looks at her baby. It is the hormone that makes you feel good (Uvnäs-Moberg et al., 2015).

TASTE

Taste is an area where humans are much more sensitive than dogs. Dogs have 1,700 taste buds; we have 9,000.

Like humans, dogs are able to taste things that are sweet, bitter, sour, and salty—just not to the same extent. For example, dogs are much less sensitive than we are to the taste of salt.

Dogs are usually very averse to bitter tastes. This is the basis of those bitter sprays you can buy to stop your dog from chewing on certain items. But be aware that these sprays may not work right away.

Your dog's bitter taste receptors are on the back of her tongue. If your dog starts to chew a pillow that has been treated with a bitter spray, she will have to really chew down on it or gnaw on it for a while before she will become aware of the bitter taste, and at this point damage may already have been done.

Also, even though their sense of taste is not as great as ours, dogs do have a couple of taste receptors that we do not.

Dogs are carnivores, and so they are very sensitive to the taste of meat and related fats. Dogs in the wild derived about 80% of their diet from meat. Even though a dog's diet today includes more fruits and vegetables, modern dogs are still drawn to meat flavors. This is why you see meat essences as key ingredients in dog food.

Dogs also have special receptors for the taste of water. Most people can not taste water at all; not dogs. Your dog tastes water on the tip of his tongue, which curls when the dog laps up water.

LIVING IN A DOG'S WORLD

Recent research describes the relationship between a dog and her person as an 'attachment,' a relationship that is very similar to that of a baby and her primary caregiver. (Siniscalchi et al., 2018). We do form very close bonds with our dogs. The danger of this kind anthropomorphic thinking, however, is that it can cause us to forget how very differently our dogs experience the world.

I often wonder what the world is like for my dog. It is fun to try and imagine.

You might start by looking at the world from the dog's point of view, close to the ground. Or you could think about the objects that make up our world and whether they mean anything, or the same thing, to you and to your dog.

For example, you might see a wooden spoon and think 'cooking'; your dog might see the same spoon but, instead, notice a wooden thing that is good to chew and even smells like food. Or you might see a disgusting pile of poop; your dog sees something good to sniff and maybe even roll in.

There are lots of things in the world that matter to us, and do not make any difference to our dogs. Other things do matter to our dogs, but either do not matter or are even unappealing to us.

What about smell? We can smell things. But, think about walking down a city street on a summer day. You will smell buses, cars and trucks; a bakery; a garbage bin. Do you also smell each of the people you are passing?

Or think about stepping outside on a crisp winter day. You take a big, deep breath, and say to yourself, "Ah, fresh air!" because you do not smell anything. Your dog would smell everything you can see, and lots of things you can not see at all.

Next time you go on a walk with your dog, try to think about the world from her point of view.

To begin with, watch her nose. She may be just standing there, but see how she holds her nose in the air and how it is working to sniff what's all around. There are smells floating in the air from near and far. Watch her snuffle on the ground. What is she noticing there?

Smelling is very different from seeing. When we use our eyes, we can immediately locate objects in the world around us. We see a wide vista and many objects in it. We especially notice things that move. As we get closer, we see lots of details. The closer we get, the more we see.

Dogs can also see objects in a wide vista of the world around them and they especially notice things that move. But a dog does not see very much detail when he gets up close. That is why he uses his nose, paws, and tongue to get information.

Young children also explore the world with fingers and mouth, but as they grow older they rely more and more on their eyes. Your dog will always be 'childlike' (or, should I say 'dog-like') in how he explores the world.

The main lesson I take from knowing how different my dog's senses are from mine is that I try to be more aware of giving him a chance to experience the world his way.

3

A DOG'S CHARACTERISTICS AND PERSONALITIES

There are many different kinds of dogs. They come in lots of shapes and sizes, with different types of fur. But, whether a Great Dane or a Chinese Crested, there are some things that all dogs have in common.

Let's start with how dogs lived in the wild. Like wolves, dogs lived in families we call packs. But dogs and wolves are not the same type of pack animal. Wolves have a pack leader but they live in egalitarian packs. All of the wolves in the pack can eat at the same time. Dogs live in hierarchical packs. Subordinate dogs do not eat at the same time as the dominant leader (Millan & Peltier, 2006).

As a result, there are some dogs that are natural leaders, but most dogs are natural followers. In the wild, the dogs who are potential leaders will respect a stronger dog as leader. In your home, they will respect you as a leader—if you take charge (I will talk more about this in Chapter 8 about communication).

When we bring a dog into our family, to the dog, we are forming a pack. Understanding a dog's natural pack instinct will help you foster a healthy relationship with your family dog.

Another thing that dogs have in common is how they eat. It is different from how we eat.

When we eat, we chew our food and that starts the process of digestion in our mouths. Watch how your dog eats her food. For dogs, digestion starts in the stomach. There is no chewing to savor the taste and break up the food for digestion!

But this is not to say that all dogs approach food the same way. Some dogs simply wolf it down. Some dogs will eat anything you put in front of them and always want more. Other dogs will eat only as much as they want and stop. But dogs only chew if something is too big to swallow.

Another thing—I have heard it said that all dogs live in the present, that they do not anticipate the future;

but I do not believe it. Dogs may not lie around wondering what is going to happen tomorrow (although if you have ever seen a dog who was abused, you might disagree), but all dogs can remember and anticipate.

A dog remembers people she met before. She fears someone who abused her, and she will have a special greeting for someone she especially likes. And it seems to me that when my dog starts asking for dinner every night at 5:30, he is anticipating a meal.

Beyond their basic dogness, however, all dogs are not alike, any more than people of a certain type are alike. Dogs vary in their ability to learn, their ability to focus, their sociability, attention span, self-control, and distractibility—in short, their personality.

EMOTION

The ancient Greeks believed that animals experienced emotion, but as religion and science developed in Western culture we came to think that only people had emotions. We know now that this is not true (Bekoff, 2000).

I think people who live with dogs have always known this. There is certainly plenty of anecdotal evidence: dogs who are joyful to be reunited with a person they have not seen for a while, or dogs who are afraid of some person or place.

Yes, dogs have emotions and science shows that a dog's emotional life operates in a way that is basically similar to ours (Coren, 2013). Like ours, the dog's emotions are connected to the limbic system—a part of the brain common to all mammals.

The limbic system activates the basic emotions. Dogs have the same neural chemistry that we do, and the same areas of their brain respond to positive and negative experiences.

Researcher Stanley Coren uses MRI technology to study and compare the brainwaves of dogs and children in situations that provoke emotion. He has found that dogs experience emotion in a way that is comparable to a two or three year old child.

Your dog experiences excitement, distress, contentment, disgust, fear, anger, joy, jealousy, suspicion/shyness and affection/love. They do not experience the more complex emotions that children learn at age three and above, such as shame, pride, guilt and contempt.

Often people attribute emotions like guilt or shame to their dogs. It is hard not to think he feels guilty when you come into the house and see that he has chewed up your shoe, and your dog hangs his head and acts like he knows he has done something wrong. But guilt implies awareness of personal wrongdoing. And the behaviors that look like guilt to us do not mean the same thing in a dog.

Coren demonstrated the difference in an experiment with a dog who was routinely getting into the kitchen trash (Coren, 2021).

The dog's people thought she knew that it was wrong for her to get in the trash because she looked guilty when they came home and found the kitchen in a mess. But Coren knew that the behaviors that the people were reading as guilt (head lowered, ears flat, tail between the legs, etc.) are actually signs of fear and submission in a dog.

To prove his point, Coren asked the dog's people to leave the house. Then he took the dog into the kitchen, where the dog watched as he tossed the trash onto the floor. The dog knew that she hadn't made the mess. But when her people came home, she still looked 'guilty' because she knew that her people would be angry when they saw the trash on the floor.

When you are training your dog, it is important to understand that your dog does not experience guilt. Your response must be immediate to the dog's action, because if you do not catch your dog in the act, he will not understand when you try to modify a behavior.

Dogs can also feel jealousy (Coren, 2011b). You may have noticed this. For example, have you ever brought home a new friend only to have your dog try to squirm between you on the couch? Does your dog try to interfere if you pet another dog?

If you have more than one dog, or if you are starting a new relationship, you will want to consider the issue of jealousy. Teach your dog to share. Make sure that dog has positive experiences when a new person is around.

Dogs also recognize and react to human emotions by paying attention to our body language and scent. This ability evolved over time, most likely because being able to read human emotions helped dogs live more successfully with us.

Dogs react to our emotions through a mechanism called 'emotional contagion,' and this ability increases for each dog the longer a dog and person live together (Katayama et al., 2019).

We see evidence of emotional contagion when a dog licks and tries to soothe someone who is unhappy or distressed. And while the effect is strongest between a dog and his person, it exists between dogs and strangers as well. You may have seen this behavior if you ever watched a therapy dog in a nursing home.

How do we recognize a dog's emotions? Since our dogs can not 'use their words,' we do this by observing the dog's body language and behavior.

There are lots of books and websites that show pictures of what dogs' emotions look like. You may want to find some that are based on your dog's physical characteristics or specific breed. But here are general things to look for that tell you how your dog is feeling:

- Happy and Friendly—relaxed stance, with ears up and tail down; eyes open and alert; normal posture; may wiggle rear end; tail up, perhaps out and wagging; may yap or give a short bark.
- Content—relaxed and likely lying down with head on front paws; may give a low moan (like a puppy), or give a sigh with eyes half closed.
- Alert—likely standing up with tail up and motionless; ears up and forward; eyes wide open; mouth closed or open but not showing teeth; in some situations the dog may whine

or give a bark.

- Assertive—alert with chest forward; ears up; tail stiff (this can also be called a dominance posture).
- Curious or Eager—may wiggle or stand on tip toe; ears up and forward; eyes open wide; mouth open with teeth covered; tail up and wagging; excited short barks and may whine or pant.
- Playful and Excited—play bow and perhaps also excited jumping up and down; ears forward and relaxed; eyes wide and sparkling; mouth relaxed; wagging tail; excited barking, whines that either stay on one pitch or drop in pitch, and panting with possible play growling.
- Anxious—body tense and in a submissive posture with tail slightly lowered or between the legs; eyes a little narrow and ears flat against head; avoids eye contact, may see whites of the eye; mouth closed or slightly open to show teeth; vocalization may include whines that rise in pitch or moan.
- Afraid—may show exaggerated anxious submission, or may have a tense submissive posture and bark and growl in warning.
- Angry or Aggressive—body stiff with weight

held forward; mouth open and teeth visible; ears back or close to head; eyes challenging; tail held straight out; fur fluffed to look as big as possible; may also bark, give a low, rumbling growl, or snarl.

In addition to showing these emotions, we also know that dogs can have emotional problems such as stress, separation anxiety, depression, or compulsive behaviors.

Many times, emotional problems for a dog are based on behavioral issues, for instance stress and separation anxiety from being left alone too long. These issues can often be addressed with training, exercise, and solutions to remove the source of the stress.

However, because dogs have brains and emotions similar to ours, they can also experience clinical mental disorders that require medication. Dogs can experience obsessive-compulsive disorders, depression, or even PTSD. Or, it is possible for some medical problems to cause behavioral symptoms.

Consult your vet if you suspect your dog has a mental disorder. We want to be alert to the mental as well as physical well-being of our dogs.

I had a friend who trained her dog, Lucy, as a therapy dog to visit people in a local nursing home. Lucy loved visiting all the residents. She performed tricks for them in the activities area and paid visits to individual rooms. She also made a particular friend of one elderly lady, Miss Julie.

Then one day Lucy went to the nursing home and trotted right up to Miss Julie's room, only to find that Miss Julie wasn't there. Miss Julie had died the previous day. Lucy was distraught and depressed. She whined miserably and turned right around to leave. In fact, she was never able to return to the nursing home again.

TEMPERAMENT

Temperament refers to behavior that is based on your dog's biology. It is not based on age, or sex, or size. It is individual to your dog and it refers to how they are naturally inclined to react in various situations.

There are three basic temperaments: assertive/aggressive, neutral, and passive.

Assertive/Aggressive

Dogs with this temperament have dominant natures. They are confident and have a high prey drive. These dogs can be territorial and possessive, and they really chew up their toys. They may act like a bully around other dogs and play rough. It takes a person who is also confident, and is willing to invest training time to help her dog moderate these qualities, in order to handle an assertive/aggressive dog.

Neutral

Dogs with a naturally neutral temperament are also confident, but their prey drive is less strong. These dogs have good coping skills. They can be very playful around other dogs, and are likely to be less destructive with their toys (but all dogs do chew!). Neutral-tempered dogs can also be good at entertaining themselves. Bad experiences or bad training can create aggression or timidity in a neutral-tempered dog, but these dogs are naturally on an even keel.

Passive

Dogs with this temperament are submissive. They lack self-confidence and have very little prey drive. They are happier to hang with you than romp in a dog park. A passive dog will avoid confrontation, and can be fearful. They are easy on toys, too. If your dog has this basic temperament, you can encourage him toward a more neutral demeanor with training, consistency and encouragement.

Temperament is described as a breed characteristic for pure-bred dogs, and this is often true. But in fact, temperament is independent of breed. You will find dogs of all temperaments in a single litter.

I have seen Rottweilers who are truly aggressive. I knew a Rottweiler, very attached to his owner, who refused to let any strangers near the house when his owner's wife got pregnant. But my own Rottweiler had a gentle, neutral temperament; and one of his littermates was very passive.

I know an adorable little Cavapoo, on the other hand, who is very assertive. She humps other female dogs, and she nips at the children in her family. Without good training, this dog will be a problem.

It is helpful to understand your dog's temperament in order to understand how best to communicate. You will need to behave differently around a dog who is naturally fearful than one who is naturally aggressive.

AGE

As with humans, age brings change to your dog. This can be very hard, especially since dogs do not live as long as we do, and having a dog means that you will inevitably have to say goodbye.

Your dog's temperament and personality stay the same, but she will slow down with age. Her muzzle will turn gray, her eyes may become cloudy, and she may develop health problems. These commonly include arthritis, dental problems, loss of vision, or loss of hearing.

A dog with arthritis will move stiffly or favor a limb. Jumping is no longer fun. He will have a hard time climbing the stairs and his back legs may be weak. An arthritic dog can also gain weight due to his decreased level of activity. This is one reason you will find special dog food formulas for the senior dog.

Dental problems, typically tartar build-up or gingivitis, can affect the dog's overall health. This is because bacteria can leach into the dog's system through plaque on the gums. One way to tell if your dog has dental issues is if she has bad breath. Having an older dog's teeth cleaned can give her a new lease on life.

Many older dogs develop lumps on their skin, which are much more noticeable on the smooth coated breeds. These lumps are usually benign, but it is a good idea to have them checked by your vet to be sure. If your dog develops lumps on his skin, you will need to be careful when grooming.

Older dogs may also need you to groom them more often because they do not groom themselves as often as they used to. An older dog's nails get brittle, which means they need to be trimmed more often.

An older dog may also develop vision or hearing loss. Blindness and deafness are not the same problem for a dog as they would be for you because your dog's primary sense is smell, but you will notice behavior changes.

One sign that your older dog is losing vision is that she may no longer care about that squirrel outside the window. She is likely to bump into things, especially if something has moved from its normal position. She may startle more easily because she does not notice things that are coming toward her. You can help a dog deal with these problems by keeping furniture in the same place and clutter off the floor.

You could even use potpourri or room freshener to give each room its own scent.

Signs that your dog has hearing loss might include failing to respond when you call, or simply being less attentive to you overall. However, dogs with hearing problems can still feel vibration and you can use this to get his attention.

Older dogs, especially dogs with short-haired coats, get cold more easily. You may need to get your older dog a coat, put more blankets on her bed, or even get a heating pad.

In extreme old age, dogs can also develop memory problems, become anxious, or become incontinent. Incontinence is often the symptom of an illness, perhaps a urinary tract infection or kidney disease. But sometimes it is simply the result of age. Your vet can tell you if there is an illness involved and, even if there is not, there are medicines that can reduce or eliminate the problem.

When you are thinking about getting a dog you should also be aware that one difference among various types of dogs is that the larger the dog, the more quickly he will age. Great Danes and Leonbergers, for instance, tend to live about eight years. They become senior citizens around age six.

Chihuahuas and Cavalier King Charles Spaniels, on the other hand, can live 15 to 20 years. They do not become senior citizens until they are 10 or older.

ENVIRONMENT MATTERS

I am sure you have heard the debate about 'nature or nurture.'

Which matters more? They both matter.

Nature is the dog's temperament and personality. Nurture is the environment in which the dog lives and grows.

Environment can have a big impact on the psychology of your dog. This goes beyond the obvious extreme of the damage that can be done by an abusive environment. A good environment is fundamental for a dog's health and well-being.

There are two components of environment. One is place:

- How large is your home—Do you live in an apartment in the city? A suburban townhouse? A farm?

- What about the people who live there—Do you live alone? In a family with children? In a space shared with roommates?
- Are there other dogs in the family? How many?
- What about where the dog exercises—Does he only get city walks? Does he play in a dog park? Is he able to run in the woods?
- What about schedule—Do you and your dog have a regular schedule? How often will the dog be on his own?

The other thing to consider about the environment involves your relationship with your dog and how well you socialize your dog.

- How many different people has your dog met?
- How many other dogs does your dog know?
- Are you able to vary the places where you walk?
- Beyond your daily walks, does the dog have opportunities to experience different places —To parks? The woods? The beach? The pet store or hardware store? Visits to other people?
- Do you take the dog in the car?

Scientists who study dogs have found that their environment can actually change a dog's brain and personality (Coren, 2008). A dog that lives in a typical family home learns faster, is less fearful, and is less stressed than a dog that spends its life in a kennel. This is because the family dog has a richer environment, with more interaction with people, more to explore, and more problems to solve.

This is why it is a good idea to socialize your dog by giving him the opportunity to experience a variety of places and meet a lot of different people.

Socialization has an impact on adult dogs and elderly dogs as well as puppies, so it is important, whether you get a puppy or adopt a shelter dog. And it continues to be important throughout your dog's life.

4

TYPES OF DOG

There are so many different dogs in the world!

I have always found that, when it was time to bring a new dog into my life, one of the great pleasures was checking out books and websites about different breeds of dog to decide what kind of dog would be right for me.

I have had dogs of all sizes. But with only one exception—my Chow Chow, Rufus—my dogs have been short-haired. And all of my dogs have had big personalities! I like a dog who lets me know what he thinks.

Many of the most popular breeds for family pets are dogs that are relatively easy to train. Many of them, like Labrador Retrievers, German Shepherds, and Golden Retrievers, have more furry coats. A family who lives with one of these dogs has to do a lot of vacuuming!

Part of thinking about getting a dog involves planning how the dog will fit into your life. If you are single, will the dog be a companion on your morning runs? Will you enjoy going on walks with the dog to meet friends for coffee? Do you want a dog to cuddle with you when you get home in the evening? Or do you work from home and want a dog who will play when you are ready, but chill when you have to work?

If you have a family with children, how old are the kids and what do they expect from the dog? Very young children are often quite rough. They do not mean to be, but like young puppies, they are still learning the limits of their strength. Your two year old son may see a furry, wiggly thing and want to grab. Your seven year old daughter may want to hug the dog and dress him up; and dogs generally do not like to be hugged. Will your dog tolerate this?

The American Kennel Club (AKC) website has a page where you can compare different breeds of dog based on things like how often they need to be groomed, how easy they are to train, how good they are with children, how much they bark, and how much exercise they need.

DOG BREEDS

Over time, dogs were bred to do different things: follow a scent, sight game, herd other animals, guard, retrieve, or chase vermin into their den. This resulted in groups of dogs with different strengths. A Bloodhound has a much better sense of smell than a Pug. A Saluki can see much farther than a Boston Terrier. A Bullmastiff is a much more intimidating guard dog than a Toy Poodle.

The AKC has divided purebred breeds into seven groups: Working, Herding, Hound, Terrier, Sporting, Non-Sporting, and Toy. The groups are based on their original function and common heritage. Dogs within each group are called a breed if you can mate them and know you will always get the same kind of dog.

Of course, there is also the 'Heinz 57'—a mongrel or mutt. A mongrel is what you get as the result of an unintentional mating between two different breeds of dog. Their mix of traits is random.

And increasingly today we are seeing so-called 'designer breeds.' These designer dogs are the result of deliberately mating two different breeds to get a dog with a certain trait or look.

I won't go into individual breeds here. If you are looking for a dog, it is fun to do the research for yourself. But I would like to talk about the nature and temperament/personality of the groups in general, because this is a window into the mind and psychology of your dog.

Working Group

Dogs in the Working Group are breeds that people created to do helpful tasks. Originally these were guard dogs, sled dogs, and herders.

One thing that everyone agrees on about these dogs is that they are large, intelligent, powerful, and protective. You need to know what you are doing if you bring a dog from the Working Group into your life.

Working dogs are also one of the most varied AKC groups and each breed has some distinct characteristics. For instance, sled dogs like Huskies or Malamutes really want to run. This means that if you take them outside off-leash, the dog is likely to dart off. She is not running away from you, she is running for the joy of it.

These dogs can be successful family pets (after all, the canine nanny in the story of Peter Pan was a Working dog: a Newfoundland). But it is important to understand that these dogs will need a job to do. Without enough activity and stimulation, they can become bored and destructive. Without proper training, they can become aggressive.

Today dogs from the Working Group are trained to do things like search and rescue and police and military work.

As I write this, the most common breeds in the U.S. from the Working Group are the Rottweiler, Pembroke Welsh Corgi, Boxer, Great Dane, and Siberian Husky (Cosgrove, 2021).

Herding Group

Herding is a job, and until 1983, herding dogs were included in the Working Group. Herding dogs were classified in their own group because, while herding is a job, there are distinctive characteristics any dog needs in order to be a good herder.

Herding dogs are able to control the movement of other animals. In the absence of cows or a flock of sheep, your herding dog will herd the family. When I was a boy, my grandfather told me about one of his friends who had an Old English Sheepdog who would come to the school to herd his boy home. (Granddad lived in a time and place where dogs were able to roam free).

There are two kinds of herding dogs: headers and heelers. A header stays at the front of a flock, using strong eye contact to control the group. The Border Collie is a header. Heelers, on the other hand, herd from the rear, often nipping at the animals' heels in order to control where they go. The Corgi is a heeler.

Herding dogs are able to do other jobs, too. For example, German Shepherds are often used in police work.

Dogs from the Herding Group are very smart and they have high energy. They are very trainable. They can also be great companions (this was a wonderful trait for shepherds and farmers who often spent a lot of time alone with their dogs). But be aware that herding dogs need plenty of exercise and someone to be in control.

The five most common Herding Group dogs in the U.S. today are the German Shepherd, Australian Shepherd, Shetland Sheepdog, Miniature American Shepherd, and Border Collie (Cosgrove, 2021).

Hounds

Hounds are hunting dogs, classified as either sight hounds or scent hounds.

Sight hounds are fast and have the sleek build of a distance runner. They will take off after anything that moves. The Greyhound, which is a sighthound, is the fastest of all dogs.

Scent hounds track with their nose. They will take off to follow a scent with single-minded purpose. Bloodhounds are the champions here, with the keenest sense of smell.

Hounds were bred to be able to work independently in the field, chasing down prey while the hunter followed, and so they have minds of their own. If you have a hound, you will need a secure yard, and you will always need to walk your dog on a leash. A hound will take off single-mindedly after an interesting sight or scent, and can easily run into traffic.

Hounds can be trained, but it is not easy.

Some hounds also do something called 'baying,' which is a kind of loud, prolonged howl. Baying made it easy to follow the dogs in the field, but not everyone likes the sound! If you are interested in getting a hound, I recommend you check to see if the breed you like is one that bays.

The five most popular hounds in the U.S. today are the Beagle, Dachshund, Basset Hound, Rhodesian Ridgeback, and Bloodhound (Cosgrove, 2021).

Terriers

Terriers come in all sizes, but they were all bred to dig to hunt vermin and other wild animal pests that live in burrows. Almost every dog in this group was originally bred in Great Britain.

Dogs in the Terrier Group are energetic and intelligent. A dog in the Terrier Group can be stubborn, feisty, and a bit of a clown. In fact, the largest terrier, the Airedale, is especially playful.

As a group, terriers tend to have rough coats. Many of them require grooming or clipping if you want to achieve a breed-standard look.

Some people say that terriers are bossy. I do not agree. To me, terriers simply know what they want and know how to make themselves clear.

The five most popular terriers in the U.S. are the Miniature Schnauzer, West Highland White Terrier, Scottish Terrier, Soft-coated Wheaten Terrier, and Airedale (Cosgrove, 2021).

Sporting Group

Sporting Group dogs are also hunters, either retrievers, pointers, setters, or spaniels.

Each type of Sporting dog works in a distinctive way:

- Retrievers bring back downed game for the hunter, either in the field or in the water. These dogs love to play fetch!
- Pointers find game and silently point toward it, standing rigid with one paw raised. They tend to have short, dense coats.
- Setters find and point, and were also bred to retrieve. These dogs have long, shiny coats that need daily brushing.
- Spaniels find and flush game, so they are likely to bark and chase after squirrels on a walk. They are gentle and have long, silky ears.

Many dogs in the Sporting Group have water-repellent coats; some have webbed feet. These dogs need lots of exercise, but they are very friendly and make great family dogs.

Unlike terriers, who work independently, sporting dogs were bred to work closely with people. They want to please and are easy to train.

The five Sporting dogs currently most popular in the U.S. are the Labrador Retriever, Golden Retriever, German Shorthaired Pointer, English

Springer Spaniel, and Brittany Spaniel (Cosgrove, 2021).

Non-Sporting Group

There is tremendous variety in the Non-Sporting Group. They come in all sizes, with all kinds of coats, and widely different personalities. Consider the Chow Chow, which is large and furry, very protective, affectionate with family, but not good with strangers. Or the French Bulldog, which is small and compact with short hair, and very friendly with family or strangers.

What Non-Sporting Group dogs seem to have in common is what they do not have in common: they were not bred to do a particular job. Sometimes, in fact, they are called the Companion Group.

With such diversity, you will need to look closely at individual breed characteristics when thinking about a dog from the Non-Sporting Group.

The five most popular Non-Sporting dogs in the U.S. today are the French Bulldog, Bulldog, Poodle, Boston Terrier, and Shiba Inu (Cosgrove, 2021).

Toy Group

Toy dogs were bred from larger cousins to be small companions. In ancient China, the first toy dog was called a 'sleeve dog' because it spent its days tucked into the sleeve of its royal owner—sort of like Paris Hilton carrying her Chihuahua around in a purse.

Toy dogs make good pets for people who live in apartments or otherwise have limited space, or for people who do not want the physical challenge of dealing with a larger dog.

Toy dogs are affectionate and have relatively low energy levels, but they tend to be better with adults and older children. Young children can be too rambunctious, especially for the smaller and more delicate dogs, which can make the dog fearful or even aggressive.

Currently, the five most popular Toy breeds in the U.S. are the Yorkshire Terrier, Cavalier King Charles Spaniel, Shih Tzu, Pomeranian, and Havanese (Cosgrove, 2021).

Mongrels

The one consistent thing about mongrels is that no two of them are alike. There can even be very different looking dogs born in the same litter. In general, however, mongrels do have multi-colored coats.

If you get a mongrel puppy, chances are you won't know who the parents were and so you can not be sure how it will look when it grows up. One rule of thumb, however, is to look at the size of the puppy's paws to gauge how big it will get.

It is possible to get a DNA test to find out the ancestry of your mongrel dog. It can be surprising to find more than a dozen breeds on the list!

I've often heard it said that mongrels are especially healthy, without the inbreeding that can cause health problems for purebred dogs. Common wisdom also says that mongrels are quite smart. This would certainly be a good survival strategy since mongrels are so often strays that must cope on their own.

The large majority of dogs in shelters are mongrels. In big cities, these are often pit bull (American Staffordshire Terrier) mixes that have a hard time finding homes. This is due to a bad reputation based on how people have used pitty mixes for fighting. It is a shame, because, although the American Staffordshire Terrier does have very strong jaws, its disposition is loving and loyal.

Bad experiences can make mongrels (like any dog) wary and distrustful, but these experiences can usually be overcome with training, love, and caring in a good home.

And as animal behaviorist Temple Grandin explains, mongrels tend to be more emotionally stable than purebred dogs, who are so often bred mainly for physical appearance. This is because selective breeding for single traits will eventually cause genetic problems (Kawczynska, 2021). You see examples of this in German Shepherds who suffer back pain because their back slopes so dramatically, or Cavalier King Charles Spaniels who are prone to heart disease (Maldarelli, 2014).

Designer Dogs

Designer dogs are the hot new thing. It seems like everyone wants some kind of a 'doodle'—maybe a Cavapoo (Cavalier King Charles Spaniel plus Poodle) or GoldenDoodle (Golden Retriever plus Poodle)— or perhaps a Puggle (Pug plus Beagle).

Poodles are often used to create designer dogs because they do not shed much and are considered hypoallergenic. Golden Retrievers are used due to their calm dispositions.

Inbreeding among AKC purebred dogs can increase recessive traits that cause health problems, such as hip dysplasia or heart problems. Some people see designer dogs as a way to address this issue.

But the results of cross-breeding are not consistent. Designer dogs aren't documented to 'breed true' (meaning three generations of producing reliably similar offspring), so there is no guarantee you will get the dog you want in terms of appearance or disposition.

It should be said that designer dogs are created by deliberate cross-breeding, just as was done when dogs were first domesticated. The problem today is that, because designer dogs are so popular, there are some unknowledgeable breeders out there. Designer dogs can have genetic problems if closely related dogs are bred together. And demand for them has spawned a lot of unscrupulous puppy mills.

The creator of the first so-called designer dog, a Labradoodle, was quoted in The *New York Times* as saying, "I opened a Pandora's box and released a Frankenstein monster," (Rueb & Chokshi, 2019).

If you want a designer dog, be sure to carefully check out the breeder and commit to giving your new dog the care and training it needs.

MATCHING DOGS TO FAMILIES

All this being said, how do you select the right dog for you and your family?

Think about whether you want a puppy or an adult dog.

Puppies are adorable, but they grow up. And do not forget housebreaking. It takes a lot of time and energy to raise a puppy, and some of the larger breeds are puppies for two years or more.

When you get an adult dog, your new dog is likely to have been spayed or neutered and may have some training, too.

Think about your lifestyle. How much time and attention will the dog need every day? How much time do you have to exercise, train, and socialize a dog? You want to be sure you have, or are able to make, room in your life to take care of the dog.

If you are a couch potato who wants a companion to snuggle with you while you binge watch the hot new series, check out lapdogs in the Toy Group. If you want a dog to help with your volunteer work in search and rescue, take a look at the Working

Group. Or a hound might be a good choice if you like to run.

There are a lot of things to consider when you are choosing a dog, and some of them may not be obvious.

The AKC describes the characteristics of each of its recognized breeds. There are many other websites, too, with questionnaires to match you with the right kind of dog.

Keep in mind, you are not looking for characteristics that are 'good' or 'bad.' You are looking for characteristics that are compatible with your lifestyle.

Experience With Dogs

To begin with, have you had a dog before? If not, a dog that is aggressive, very high energy, or hard to train may not be a good choice. You can get one of these dogs, but you will need to be clear that you can handle the amount of training, exercise, and activity such a dog needs.

First-time dog owners are more likely to have a good experience with a dog that is affectionate, easy to train, and eager to please.

Environment

Think about where you live and what this will mean for your dog and you. All dogs need plenty of space to play—the larger the dog, the larger the space. The dog will need daily walks. Your dog will also need to be socialized, and your environment will affect opportunities to socialize the dog and give him new experiences.

Do you live in an apartment, a townhouse, or a detached house? In the city, the suburbs, a small town, or the country?

How much room do you have indoors for the dog to play? Do you have a fenced yard? How big is your yard? Where will you go to take the dog for walks?

Family

Are you single? Do you have a partner? Do you have children and, if so, how old are they? All of these considerations will help you decide what kind of dog will be a good fit for the family.

Some people with young children, for example, like the idea of getting a puppy to grow up with the kids. This can be wonderful; it is what happened for me. But you need to be sure that you have a dog that is good with kids—who will tolerate, and even enjoy, the rough and tumble without getting aggressive.

What about pets? Do you have another dog, a cat, birds, a hamster?

A dog with a strong prey drive may not be a good match in a house with other small pets. A young puppy may not be a good match in a house with another, senior dog. If you are thinking about a second dog, make sure the two dogs' energy levels and temperaments are a match. This is more important than matching them in size.

Energy and Activity Level

All dogs need exercise and stimulation, but some need much more than others.

Would you like a dog to run with you while you are training for a marathon? Would you like a dog that will be happy with a good daily walk? Or would you be happier with a calm couch potato?

Be realistic and match the dog's energy level to the amount of exercise you can guarantee to provide. A dog who does not get enough exercise can become destructive very quickly.

Activity level is important, too, especially with Working, Herding, and Sporting breeds. These dogs were bred to have a job to do and are often quite smart. You will need to provide stimulating activities to keep the dog from getting bored (more about that in Chapter 6).

And also consider how much time your dog will spend alone. All dogs are social animals and will want, in fact, need to spend time with you every day; but some dogs are more independent than others.

If your dog will be alone a lot, take a look at a Basset Hound, Greyhound, Whippet, Chihuahua, French Bulldog, Maltese or Shar Pei. You may be surprised to find fast-running dogs like Greyhounds and Whippets on this list, but these dogs alternate bursts of great energy with a lot of sleep. And especially if you adopt a former racing Greyhound, you will be getting a dog that is used to being alone in a kennel all day.

On the other hand, if your dog is going to be alone all day, do not consider a Working dog like a Border Collie. Even the popular Labrador Retriever may not be the best dog for that situation.

Barking

Dogs bark, but some dogs bark a lot more than others.

In my experience, a Jack Russell Terrier likes to let you know what he is thinking with a bark. My

Doberman, on the other hand, was a pretty quiet fellow.

Consider how you will feel if you have a dog who barks at everything that happens outside on the street. Or, is it likely that your dog will bark when he is left alone in the house? The neighbors won't like that.

Dogs bark if they are feeling protective or territorial. They bark to get attention, or when they are playing. They might bark from fear, boredom, or loneliness.

Check to see how much the dog you want is likely to bark, and do not get a dog you know will be more vocal than you want. You can train a dog to keep barking to a minimum, but this takes time and patience. And do not expect to stop all barking, all the time.

Grooming

Some dogs are fluffy fur balls, others are smooth and sleek. Some dogs shed seasonally; others shed all the time. All dogs shed, just as all people shed hair. But dogs with different coats will shed different amounts, and they require different types of care.

A St. Bernard with thick fur will shed a lot more than a smooth-coated dog like a Weimaraner. So, ask yourself how much vacuuming you are prepared to do.

Dogs with different coats also need different amounts of regular grooming. Brushing your dog can be a good bonding experience. But grooming takes time, and if you cannot do it yourself, it can be expensive.

You do not have to groom your dog to look like one of the dogs at the Westminster dog show, but you will have to make sure her coat does not get matted because that can cause skin problems.

You will also need to take care of your dog's nails, teeth, and ears. As with their coat, these needs vary with the type of dog—especially the ears. Dogs with long, floppy ears can be prone to ear infections.

Size

How much dog can you handle? Dogs range greatly in size, from the tiny Teacup Yorkie to the pony-sized Tibetan Mastiff. It is not just a matter of whether the dog is the right size to sit in your lap. Consider, too, how strong the dog will be. Will you be able to control your dog when walking on a leash? Do you live in a place where the dog will have enough room to stretch her legs? Or, will you be in danger of tripping over a tiny dog you do not see on the floor?

I had a colleague at work who always said she wanted a big dog that she did not have to lean over to pet. But when she retired and wanted to get a dog, she looked for a medium-sized dog that she knew she could handle instead.

Trainability

Any dog can be trained, but some of them are tough customers!

It is important to train your dog, no matter the size. Even a tiny dog can be a pest if it does not have good manners. A well-behaved dog will sit and not jump on people, walk nicely on a leash, and come when you call.

These things are easier, though, for some dogs than for others. Just one example is the come command. It is easier to teach this to a sporting dog, which was bred to work closely with his human, than to a hound, which was bred to range far away.

Beyond good manners, is training something you want to do with your dog? Training can be a real pleasure with a working or herding dog that really wants a job to do.

5

HOW A DOG LEARNS

It is fascinating to look into the mind of a dog.

Talking about a dog's senses as we did earlier opens a window on the question of how a dog's mind works, because the ability to think and learn depends, at least in part, on the information available.

What do your dog's senses tell him?

We know that the dog's acute sense of smell makes it possible for him to sense emotion based on the pheromones, the chemical signature, that you, and other animals, release. Your dog will sense your emotions even if you are trying to suppress and control what you feel. For this reason, how you are feeling while you are training a dog affects what the dog learns.

We know that a dog's superior ability to detect motion makes her sensitive to what you do while you are speaking to her.

A functional MRI study conducted in 2018 found that verbal commands were significantly less effective in dog training than either hand signals or olfactory stimuli (Prichard et al., 2018).

For this reason, trainers often use hand signals together with verbal commands. Hand signals are also how dog actors can be trained to hear one command and perform another, such as when an actor says "sit" and the dog lies down.

In addition to sensory input, the ability to think also depends on how the brain works. We know that a dog's brain is different, and that as a result dogs do not have language as we know it. They do not use words and symbols the way we do to think and communicate.

Temple Grandin is a professor of animal sciences. She is also autistic and, from her personal experience, has interesting insights into how lack of language affects the way animals think.

Grandin explains that autistic people like her do not think in language, they think in pictures (Kawczynska, 2021). Instead of forming concepts by naming things and creating a generic mental image of them as a category, people who think in pictures form concepts by remembering many different instances of various things and picking out visual similarities. For example, Grandin formed the concept "dog" by thinking of all the different kinds of dogs she had seen and realizing that they all have a dog-like nose.

I do not know, but perhaps dogs do the same thing. And I ask myself if they also use their more acute senses, such as smell and hearing, to develop concepts.

Despite the difference, though, we know that dogs do think. They have desires and take action to get what they want. They are able to solve problems, which means that they can do at least some level of planning.

Psychologist Stanley Coren has a great story about how a dog plans. Coren's flat-coated retriever, Odin, wanted to be taken for a walk on a cold, wet day. First the dog brought Coren his leash. When that did not work, he brought him one shoe, and then the other. When that did not work, Odin went to the door and gave the kind of bark he only used to mean "Your wife is coming home. Unlock the door!" It wasn't true, but once Coren was at the door, Odin did get his walk (Coren, 2017).

I think anyone who has lived with a dog has similar anecdotal evidence of things their dogs do to get what they want. But these stories focus on immediate situations rather than long-range planning.

This is why dog trainers say that you need to communicate with your dog based on the immediate situation. You can not use your words to connect what you do now to something you can not describe in the future.

We also know that different dogs have differing capacities to learn. Some dogs pay more attention to the people around them; other dogs pay more attention to the environment. Some dogs learn quickly, it almost seems by osmosis (like a child who learns to read by being read to). Other dogs require more structured instruction for even the most basic commands.

Dogs do have good memories, though. As you watch your dog you will notice that she learns to know the neighborhood, she remembers people, and she remembers things that happened to her (both good and bad).

SOCIAL LEARNING AND OBSERVATION

Learning to Be a Dog

Your dog's first teachers are her mother and littermates.

The mother starts the process of socialization. It begins with a basic communication exchange (puppy cries, mother responds). The mother's demeanor also teaches her pups about how to respond to the world. The more calm she is, the more relaxed and calm her puppies will be.

One way a very young puppy can misbehave is to bite too hard. The mother starts to teach bite inhibition by moving away from a puppy if it is biting her. The lesson continues as puppies grow and play with littermates. They learn about boundaries: not to bite too hard and not to play too rough. They also gain coordination and dexterity.

This early period of socialization is very important. A dog's health can be compromised if it is taken away from its mother before it is ready to be weaned at seven or eight weeks. There can be behavioral effects, too. Puppies taken away from their mother and littermates too soon can develop problems like anxiety, aggression, destructiveness, or house-breaking issues.

Some people recommend that puppies stay with their mother and littermates for three months, but this does not happen very often. Most people who want a puppy do not want to miss out on that adorable baby stage, and puppies can do well if they come to their new home after being weaned.

Learning to Know People

The breeder also plays an important role in a puppy's first weeks of life. A good breeder will handle each puppy every day, gently stroking them at least twice a day so the puppy learns the pleasure of human touch.

Good breeders will also provide a stimulating environment for puppies that are old enough to leave the whelping box. This means providing toys to chew, climb over, and run through. The breeder may even start the training process.

There is another kind of socialization that some breeders do called Early Neurological Stimulation (ENS). ENS was developed by the U.S. Military as a way to prepare puppies for training as military working dogs.

ENS consists of a series of five short exercises that are done once a day, starting when a pup is three days old and continuing until day sixteen. As reported on the AKC website, puppies who experienced properly conducted ENS had stronger hearts, were more disease resistant, and were better able to cope with stress. ENS puppies were also more active and exploratory, so their learning was improved (Leigh, 2021).

ASSOCIATION (CLASSICAL CONDITIONING)

Learning by association is involuntary. When two things happen at the same time, your dog will associate one with the other. This is the classical kind of conditioning described by psychologist Ivan Pavlov when he taught dogs to salivate at the ringing of a bell. He did this by ringing a bell each time they were fed.

When you pick up the leash and then go for a walk, your dog learns that leash means walk. If she then jumps around in excitement, you need to teach her to sit or wait to moderate that enthusiasm.

Perhaps when you go to the food canister, your dog starts to drool because he knows that dinner is coming. That is learning by association, too.

Learning by association can be a good thing—or not...

It is helpful when you are able to teach your dog by repeated experience that the environments they will encounter are good.

On the other hand, one way learning by association may cause a problem is if you have a routine and the routine needs to change. For example, what if you feed your dog every day at 5:00 p.m. Then your schedule changes and you can not feed him until 6:00 or 7:00 p.m. Or what if you were working from home when you got your dog, but now have to be away from the house for work for 9-10 hours a day. These kinds of changes will pose some real issues for folks who got Covid puppies!

OPERANT CONDITIONING

Operant conditioning is the process of deliberately linking a behavior and a consequence.

The consequence might be positive: when I sit, I will get a reward. The consequence can also be negative:

if I growl and act aggressive when I am playing tug, my person will stop playing and take the toy away.

Food is the reward most often used in training; but there are dogs that are more motivated by praise or by a favorite toy than by food. Your dog will quickly show you what matters most to him.

We call this positive and negative reinforcement. Negative reinforcement shouldn't mean punishment or pain. You do not want to use force to train your dog any more than you want to use spanking as a way to teach your kids. Negative reinforcement simply means an undesirable consequence.

Punitive negative reinforcement used to be the standard way to teach a dog. Trainers used a metal 'choke collar' and pulled on the chain whenever the dog did not do the right thing. In my grandparents' day, it was said that the best way to housetrain a puppy was to put the puppy's nose in the mess, smack it with a rolled up newspaper, and put the puppy outside whenever they found a puddle on the floor.

We now know that positive reinforcement is a much more effective method (Vieira de Castro et al., 2020). For example, when the organization Guide Dogs for the Blind changed its methods from negative techniques to positive reinforcement they found that training time was cut in half and the dogs were able to work an extra year or two because they were less stressed (Ross, 2020).

You can use operant conditioning to teach your dog commands and tricks, and also how to be okay with things they do not like. I learned this with my Miniature Pinscher, who absolutely hated to have his nails clipped. What I did was give him a high value treat (his favorite food) while clipping his nails, and he soon learned that nail clipping was okay.

Know your dog, and make sure the rewards you use are things that are valuable to that dog.

6

ENCOURAGING GOOD BEHAVIOR

Dogs benefit from the same standards and expectations for good behavior that we give to our children.

Some experts recommend that you always think of

your dog as about two years old in human terms. This can be helpful. It does address some of what we know about how a dog's brain is structured and works.

Children thrive in a world with structure, limits, expectations, and rules that are consistently enforced. Dogs do, too.

Cesar Millan, who became famous on National Geographic's show *The Dog Whisperer*, has spent a lifetime with dogs. As a child in Mexico, he roamed over the family farm with the family pack of dogs. He now lives in the United States and specializes in handling dogs with serious behavior problems.

Millan talks about a key difference in experience between human and canine babies—how puppies need to go to the mother dog to nurse. A human mother will hear her baby cry and come get the baby to nurse. A mother dog will come to the den or whelping box, but does not come directly to the puppies. From the beginning, the dominant creature —this time the mother—lets the other dogs come to her.

Millan recommends that we can establish our leadership position by behaving in a similar way. When we treat dogs like babies and humanize them, it can get in the way of encouraging their good behavior. For example, here are some tips Millan recommends for establishing our leadership position:

- Do not let your dog be first when going out the door.
- Do not let the dog be in charge when on the leash.
- Do not let the dog jump on you, or anyone.
- Do not let the dog tell you when to wake up or when to feed him.

In Chapter 3, in the section on emotion, I talked about an assertive posture. You will see this demeanor when your dog is trying to get you to do something. But just because your dog tells you something and you understand, does not mean you have to say yes.

Do not be fooled here by language (dominant/submissive). Dominance does not mean whips and chains. It does not mean punitive training techniques. Dominance in this context means calm and confident direction.

It is important for humans to take the leadership role because we expect dogs to live in our world, and we know the rules.

The issue is behavior. We know how we want our dogs to behave.

If we understand why our dogs are acting a certain way, we will be better able to deal with the behavior. Dogs are sentient creatures. When your dog does something, it is doing so for a reason.

The fundamental way to encourage good behavior is to make sure your dog has what he needs: exercise, leadership, and love. Then look for something that is getting in the way of the behavior you want.

Dogs need to exercise both their bodies and their minds. A good daily walk does both.

Some folks will tell you that, when you are walking your dog, you need to keep the dog beside you and walk briskly, stopping only so the dog can relieve himself. This kind of walk might be great for you, if your purpose is getting in those steps or miles. But it ignores your dog's desire to explore and engage his mind. So give the dog a chance to do both.

You don't want the dog to pull. But it is fine to stop for a sniff about.

What can you do if you have a high energy dog and can not give him enough physical exercise? Consider hiring a dog walker; try using a treadmill; or put a backpack on the dog so he uses more energy during your walk.

What about mental exercise? As we have discussed, many dogs—especially those from the Working, Herding, and Sporting Groups—really need something to do. One solution is to train your dog for a special activity or job. And on a daily basis, provide this kind of dog with stimulating toys for when you are not around.

PROBLEM BEHAVIORS

Aggression

Aggression is a serious problem. If it is out of control, someone is likely to be badly hurt. So one of the most important things you can do for your dog is to help her avoid the problem of aggression.

There are two reasons a dog might become aggressive: dominance or fear.

Some dogs are just naturally more dominant than others—like some people are naturally more bossy. These dogs simply need to understand who calls the shots.

The potential for dominance issues to get out of hand is why some trainers tell you never to play tug or roughhouse with your dog. But as you know, these are things that dogs really like. So if you do play tug or roughhouse, be alert for signs of dominance. If the dog starts acting possessive (growling, snarling, or snapping), it is time to stop.

Some dogs, no matter their natural disposition, can become aggressive due to fear—just like even the most mild-mannered person can reach a point where they push back.

Fear might be caused by abuse, a frightening experience or—most often, by lack of socialization. The dog may be afraid of being groomed, of unfamiliar dogs or people (especially children), or loud noises, like the vacuum cleaner or fireworks. Fear can be a problem with little dogs, especially around children who do not yet know their own strength.

Fear aggression looks a little different than dominance aggression. It starts with the dog's ears back, showing her teeth, snarling, or exhibiting 'whale-eye' (showing the white of the eye). Nipping behavior can follow. Or a fearful dog might cower into a defensive posture.

The best solution for you and your dog is to prevent the problem of aggression from developing. However, if aggression is a problem, how should you handle it?

If the aggression is more dominance-related and happens during play, calmly disengage. Wait until the dog quiets down before you return to play. If the dog does not settle down, give him a time out in a quiet place. If you know that certain types of play stimulate aggression, avoid that kind of play.

If the aggression is caused by fear: do not stare at the dog. Do not try to comfort her with cuddling, or reach out to pat her head, because she may see these actions as aggression. Back off and give the dog time to calm down. Do your best to project the feeling that everything is OK.

It is also important to consult your vet or a good dog trainer for help if aggression problems persist.

Separation Anxiety

Dogs who have problems being alone can develop separation anxiety. When this happens, you will come home to a mess. The dog becomes destructive and may even urinate or defecate in the house.

Before talking about separation anxiety in adult dogs, we should talk about how to handle teaching a young dog to be alone.

Your dog needs to learn how to be alone when you are gone just as a child needs to learn how to go to sleep alone in bed at night. But of course, it is important not to leave your dog alone for too long a time.

As anyone knows who has brought a young puppy home, your puppy will need to go outside a lot: right away when she first gets up from a nap, after play, after eating, after drinking—pretty much every couple hours or so.

As the puppy gets older, they have more control. The rule of thumb is that you can leave a puppy alone for as many hours as it is months old, because that is the limit of how long puppies can go between bathroom breaks.

Crate training is one good way to handle this. The crate limits the area where the dog might make a mess, and you also teach the dog to relax in the quiet and safety of the crate. Even if you do not use a crate, when you leave your dog alone, it is a good idea to limit the dog to a relatively small area where they will be safe and can not do too much damage.

My dog, Max, has a crate. When we travel, if I can not bring the crate along, I often put his travel carrier in a closet and use the closet for a kennel. I know people who use an exercise pen set up in a basement corner, or a baby gate to block off a room.

Teach the puppy to handle being alone by gradually increasing how long you are gone. By the time your dog is ten months old, he will be able to be alone for an entire work day without needing to relieve himself.

When you bond with your dog, you form an attachment. This needs to be a healthy relationship. We often feel guilty about leaving our dogs, because we understand that they want our company. But something to keep in mind when you think about leaving your dog alone is that dogs sleep a lot.

Young puppies sleep as much as 20 hours a day. An adult dog sleeps about 12 hours a day. Senior dogs sleep more.

Some dogs like it if you leave the radio on. I've heard of folks leaving the TV on, too, but that uses a lot of electricity.

The important thing, I think, is for you to be calm and confident when you say goodbye. If you are feeling anxious and guilty, the dog will pick up on how you feel.

Every dog needs to be able to be alone for a reasonable amount of time. If you go out to work every day, your dog needs to be able to handle it.

The problem is, especially if you are going to be gone all day, the dog won't be asleep the entire time. Being shut up in a crate or kennel, or even given the run of the house, does not offer the dog a good way to use up all of its natural energy. Each dog's needs vary based on breed and personality, but dogs are living creatures and they need something to do.

Destructive behaviors such as chewing up your shoes, the sofa, or the drywall are caused by boredom.

The Boredom Beast

Your dog needs to learn how to amuse himself appropriately.

You can encourage this by keeping an eye on how your dog is behaving when crated or kenneled, and letting her out at a time when she is playing quietly on her own. You may think that interrupting her quiet play will discourage the behavior, but in fact, letting the dog out to be with you at a time when she is doing something that you like is classical conditioning—a good way to encourage more of that behavior.

Some dogs will be satisfied by having one or two favorite toys. Other dogs need more stimulating activity. There are a number of activity toys you might try. They all involve hiding food for the dog to get out. Some, like the Kong, are easy—simply tuck food inside the mouth of the Kong. Others are puzzles for the dog to solve.

Hyperactivity

Hyperactivity is another problem a dog may have when he doesn't get enough exercise.

Hyperactivity is overexcitement caused by pent up energy. Your dog will seem to be bouncing off the walls!

The amount of exercise your dog needs will be based on the breed and energy level of the dog. Basset Hounds are fine with a daily walk around the block. Weimaraners like to walk four or five miles a day, with some real runs or hikes on the weekend.

Part of living with a dog is making sure your dog gets enough exercise before you leave for the day.

Cesar Millan talks about the importance of giving your dog the right kind of exercise—walking or running rather than a long game of fetch. He compares playing fetch to taking your kids to Chuck E. Cheese's, a frenetic activity that can make them overexcited. Walking, on the other hand, he compares to taking piano lessons, an activity that engages the mind and body (Millan & Peltier, 2006).

Some people do not have the time or ability to give their dog the walks they need every day. There may be someone else in the family who can pick up the slack. If not, or if it is just you, a dog walker or even a kid in the neighborhood who wants to make a few bucks can be a big help.

SPEND TIME TOGETHER

Dogs are social creatures. The desire to be with people is one of the characteristics that became part of dogs with domestication.

When you get a dog, your dog will form a bond with you and want to be with you. So when you bring a dog into your life, you are making a commitment to take care of it, and that means spending time together.

In fact, if you are thinking about getting a dog but know this is going to be a problem, consider whether the time is right for you to bring a dog into your life. Having a dog when you aren't able to spend time together is not fair for either of you!

You will be together on exercise walks and just being at home relaxing at the end of the day. For some low-energy dogs, that is enough. A lapdog is happy to be with you. But for other, high-energy dogs, you will need to be more actively involved.

As with the daily walk, what this means for you personally depends on the size of your family. In a family with young kids, for example, even if you are the primary caregiver for meals and daily walks, there will be other people around to romp and play with the dog.

But if it is just you and you have a high-energy dog in your life, look for ways to involve your dog in your normal activities. For example, if your dog likes to ride in the car, take the dog along when you go shopping. Or if you like to meet friends for a cup of coffee, there are plenty of coffee shops with outdoor cafes that welcome canine guests. My local coffee shop even puts out bowls of water and treats for canine customers.

There are also plenty of dog-specific activities such as going to a dog park, setting up a doggy play date, or taking a training class.

IT WON'T BE CUTE WHEN THEY'RE GROWN UP

One of the most common pitfalls if you are getting a new dog, especially if you are getting a puppy and have never had a dog before, is to excuse behavior that is adorable when they are small but becomes annoying—or even dangerous—as the dog grows up.

The simplest example is jumping. Puppies are tiny and it is not a problem if they jump up on you. It is even cute that they are so glad to see you. But when that 8 pound puppy becomes an 80 pound Labrador, jumping up is not so cute any more!

The fact is, do not let your adorable puppy do anything that you do not want her to do when she is grown up.

It is hard. They're awfully cute and they do not really know what they are doing. But that is the point. They do not know what they are doing, and it is up to you to tell them.

7

UNDERSTANDING WHAT YOUR DOG SAYS TO YOU

Why is my dog acting like that?

In Chapter 3 I talked a little about how your dog's posture and vocalization let you know what she is feeling. Everything your dog does can tell you something.

Dogs communicate consciously and unconsciously, using body language and sound. How you interpret what she is saying will vary depending on the situation. For instance, a wagging tail does not always mean 'happy.'

The Tufts School of Veterinary Medicine website categorizes canine communication into five groups: relaxed, excited, anxious, fearful, and aggressive (Dog Communication and Body Language, 2022).

Tufts describes these communications for future vets who will be dealing with dogs they do not know. As you and your dog get to know each other, you will come to understand what your dog is saying and also develop a special language of your own.

FIVE TYPES OF COMMUNICATION

Relaxed and Confident

It is easy to tell when your dog is relaxed.

When relaxed, your dog's posture is open to the world around her. Her eyes and muscles are soft, her mouth may be slightly open and tongue loose. She may seem to be smiling.

When a relaxed dog is lying down, you might see her flat on her belly in what's called a 'frog-leg' position, or a 'sploot'. She will have all four feet splayed out, front legs pointing forward and back legs pointing back.

A dog who is confident when not lying down will stand up fully with head erect. You can see the dog is ready for what comes. If he is even leaning a little forward, the dog is alert and on the watch.

Excited

Some signs that your dog is excited include jumping, mouthing, or even mounting. Mouthing can become biting if it is not corrected. Both male and female dogs can exhibit mounting behavior.

And, of course, sometimes when your dog is excited he will tell you 'let's play!' He will put his chin on the ground and stick his butt in the air in the classic play bow. It is an invitation.

At other times when he is excited, your dog's fur may stand up, especially the hackles along his back. His ears will be forward. His body will be held at the ready, with tail up and wagging and eyes wide open and focused. Some dogs will also bark or lunge.

Anxious

When your dog is anxious, he won't be able to focus; and if the anxiety continues, he may become fearful.

An anxious dog's posture is a little lowered. His ears are back a little. If his tail is wagging, it wags slowly.

The dog may have one of two levels of activity, depending on the dog and the situation.

At one level, anxiety can cause a dog to withdraw or become detached from his surroundings. Your dog may yawn when he is not tired or lick his lips when he is not hungry. He may drool.

At the other level, he may get over-excited. Anxious excitement can cause your dog to pace, spin around or pant. Anxious panting happens when the dog hasn't been running around and it is not very hot.

Fearful

A dog usually reacts to fear with her entire body. She will tense her body and cower, perhaps tucking her tail and putting her ears back. A fearful dog crouches, with head down, in order to avert anger or aggression. The more fearful she becomes, the more of these behaviors you will see and the more exaggerated her actions will become.

If the fear is not extreme, the dog may lie down and show her belly. She is saying, "You are the boss."

As with anxiety, you may see her licking her lips or yawning, although eventually a fearful dog will keep her mouth tightly closed.

She may start to tremble, avoid eye contact, and orient herself away from whatever is scaring her.

Excessive fear can make a dog aggressive.

Aggressive

Dogs naturally express aggression as a way to avoid or de-escalate a situation. Most dogs prefer to avoid a fight, and an aggressive display between two dogs usually ends when one of the dogs backs down.

However, a dog that has not been well socialized—either to people or to other dogs—can be aggressive and confrontational. These dogs simply lack good communication skills.

When a dog expresses aggression, it is situational. The behavior may be caused by fear, a perceived threat, or a desire to protect something. Aggressive behavior starts with a warning meaning something like 'keep away,' 'back off,' or 'this is mine.'

When a dog feels aggressive, you will see that her body is stiff. She may freeze with mouth tensed or lips curled. Her eyes will be wide so that you will see a 'whale eye.' And she will likely bark or growl.

One common time to see aggressive/possessive behavior is when your dog is gnawing a bone or chewing on a favorite toy. He may growl or bare his teeth. This is why we tell children never to try to take food away from a dog or grab a toy out of a dog's mouth. However, it is a bad idea to allow this kind of behavior and we will talk about how to train your dog not to be possessive in the next chapter.

If aggressive signals are combined with signs of fear, the dog may feel compelled to act beyond just growling or baring teeth. The result can be snapping, biting, or even an attack with tooth and claw.

Aggressive behavior is of concern between dogs and people, and also between two or more dogs. Between dogs it can happen when you are out walking or at a dog park. Or it can happen between dogs living in the same house. If you have more than one dog and they are starting to fight it is a good idea to consult a vet.

BODY LANGUAGE

Beyond understanding your dog's five basic types of communication, there are lots of things they tell us all the time. Here are some common body language communications.

A Talking Tail

Yes, your dog wags her tail when she is happy. But over time you will notice that your dog's tail wags in many different ways, and that wagging does not always mean that the dog is happy. Here are some different ways dogs communicate with their tail:

- The speed and vigor of the wag indicates intensity of emotion.
- When your dog is excited to see you, she will get 'helicopter tail', wagging her tail vigorously around in circles.
- If the dog is feeling defensive or aggressive, she will hold her tail high and wag it stiffly.
- If the tail is drooping and the wag is quick, the dog is showing you submission.
- A lightly wagging tail is an indication of interest.
- A lively tail is a sign of high interest.
- A slowly wagging tail might indicate either fear or submission.
- If your dog is holding her tail still, she is likely paying close attention to something.

Of course, different dog breeds have different kinds of tails: straight or curly, furry or smooth, long or short. A few dogs, like the Pembroke Welsh Corgi, do not really have tails at all, just a flap of fatty tissue that they can wave.

Different dogs naturally hold their tails in different positions—think of a beagle with her tail like a flag behind him or a greyhound with her tail curved low. You will read your dog's tail differently based on the kind of tail she has, but here are some rules of thumb for a typical dog:

- When she is feeling confident, alert or excited, she will hold her tail in the air.
- When she is relaxed, the dog's tail is in a neutral position (which will vary from dog to dog).
- When a dog is feeling insecure, fearful, or being submissive, she will hold her tail low.

Tail language is harder to read if your dog's tail is docked. Docking is a surgical procedure to shorten the tail of a sporting or working breed like the Weimaraner or Cocker Spaniel. This practice is discouraged by veterinarians today, especially as it appears to be done for purely cosmetic reasons. In England, the practice is now banned (AVMA Staff, n.d.).

A Speaking Face

We read a lot in our dog's faces. Sometimes their expressions look so human! But we can not entirely rely on these similarities.

When your dog cocks her head to one side and looks at you when you talk, this gesture is similar to ours.

It means the dog is listening and trying to understand.

When your dog is holding her mouth open and showing her teeth, it can look like a grin. But really, depending on the situation, when her mouth is open like that, she is either saying that she is excited or that she is stressed. The wider the grin, the stronger the emotion.

Your dog can also yawn. But dogs do not yawn from boredom. Instead a yawn means anxiety or stress. Yawning also seems to help the dog calm down.

Human breeding programs over the years have affected the abilities of some breeds of dogs. Dogs like pugs, with short skulls and flat faces, are not able to communicate fully with their faces. Other dogs have been bred to have permanently erect ears, which affects their ability to communicate in that way.

Dogs also communicate with eye contact, but they do this differently with humans than they do with other dogs (Siniscalchi et al., 2018).

Between dogs, steady eye contact is used to establish dominance or make a challenge. This is why you should avoid staring at a dog who is frightened or seems unfriendly.

Between humans, eye contact can be a challenge. But it has other meanings, too. We've talked about eye contact that conveys a surge of love. Eye contact is also used to open a connection, or direct attention. And domestic dogs have learned to make eye contact with us in similar ways.

There was an experiment done to determine whether domestic dogs use their gaze to communicate with humans more than wild dogs would do. Animal psychologist Akitsugu Konno and his research team studied 120 pet dogs of 26 breeds, classifying them according to their genetic similarity to wolves. The idea was that the older breeds would use gaze less to communicate with humans and, in fact, this was shown to be the case (Konno et al., 2016).

All of the dogs looked toward the humans when presented with a treat that was out of reach. However, the more ancient breeds of dog were significantly less likely to look toward humans when they were tasked to get a treat out of a container that they couldn't open.

The less like a wolf, the more the dog was inclined to use eye contact to communicate with humans. The use of eye contact was also shown to be a learned behavior based on the fact that older dogs used eye contact more than younger ones. The researchers also cited a related study showing that household dogs use eye contact more than shelter dogs.

And as anyone who has ever lived with a dog knows, communicating with a look is a two way street. Dogs gaze at us to get our attention—sitting at our feet and gazing up soulfully. They can also use their gaze to direct our attention—sitting on the kitchen floor and gazing steadily at the treats jar.

Greeting

We love it when our dogs are excited to see us, and it can be hard to discourage their joy—especially if it is a puppy or a tiny dog. Too much excitement, though, can be off-putting. And other people may not be as thrilled as you are to get an exuberant doggy hello.

When your dog is meeting someone new, it is a good idea to help manage the situation by making sure that the other person understands the best way to meet a new dog. It is different from meeting another person.

We greet another person by looking right at them, saying, "Hello," and perhaps also shaking hands.

When greeting an unfamiliar dog, however, this natural human instinct is not appropriate. Tell the new person not to approach the dog. Instead, they should hold out one hand and let the dog make the first move. Do not force the dog, but if she is reluctant you can give the person a treat to hold out. If she barks a warning, do not force the issue. And keep an eye on your dog's body language to make sure she is not getting scared.

This can be a challenge with young children, who want to rush right in with a pat on the head or a hug. I've found that it works to tell a child, "The dog is shy. Why don't you give her a treat instead?"

Sometimes you will see a dog raise his paw when he is looking at someone new. This does not mean he is asking to shake hands. It means he is a little anxious. Since dogs stand on all four feet, raising one foot off the ground is actually a sign of submission. A good response would be for the new person to use a friendly voice to say hello.

Dogs can startle just like people do if they are touched and do not see it coming. This can be a problem in a home with young children if the children overwhelm the dog, because this can lead to defensive behavior that can be dangerous.

Some people are embarrassed by the way dogs want to greet people by sniffing their genital area, or even when they sniff another dog's. We can restrain our dogs and teach them not to do this to other people, but sniffing is a natural greeting between dogs. When two dogs greet each other there is a ritual of touching noses, sniffing mouths, and sniffing under the tail.

Why do they do this? It is to get a good whiff of the other dog's scent signature. From scent, your dog will learn the other dog's emotional state as well as things like age, health, what he had for dinner, and where he has been.

Mounting

Something else that dogs do that can be embarrassing to people is mounting, or humping. Mounting is a natural and necessary part of sex. But it is also something both male and female dogs might do when they are excited.

Puppies mount each other in play to say "I'm boss." As they get older, female dogs may hump other female dogs. Sometimes a dog will hump a person's leg or even hump their bed. This behavior can be a sign of social dominance, emotional arousal, overexcitement, or even boredom.

If this happens just once in a while, do not worry. If the behavior is excessive, redirect your dog to other activities and help her calm down. If the mounting behavior is accompanied by distress signals such as licking or chewing, you may want to see the vet (Robins, 2019).

Scent Marking

To a person, this simply looks like peeing, but to a dog it is communication.

When you are out on a walk, you will notice your dog sniffing trees and posts and spots on the ground. This is because dogs do not only urinate to relieve their bladder. They use urine to mark territory and announce their presence. Male dogs, when they lift their leg, often spray urine as high up as they can, making it more difficult to mark over. Some female dogs even try to do the same.

Another thing a dog will do after urinating is paw the ground. This transfers scent from their paws and also disperses the scent on the air.

Licking

The first thing a mother dog does when her puppies are born is lick them to stimulate breathing and get the puppies moving. And she licks them as she cares for them every day. Puppies in turn will lick around their mother's mouth as a signal of submission.

Adult dogs use licking too. They might lick another dog or their human caregiver to signal submission or appeasement.

My dog, Max, likes to lick me in the morning to say hello.

Dogs will also lick to clean a wound or to relieve pain in an area with no obvious wound. I had a dog who kept licking her paw, which looked okay, but when I took her to the vet it turned out that there was a cut hidden deep between her toes that had become infected. It got treated and the dog was fine.

Zoomies

Sometimes, especially when he is young, it may seem that your dog is going a little crazy, running pell-mell around the house. He has the zoomies.

This is normal behavior to release energy. Just like young children, young dogs have a lot of energy. They need it for all the physical and mental exertion it takes to grow and learn; if you are not able to give your dog enough exercise and stimulation, the dog will still need a way to let off steam.

This is normal, but if your dog is zooming around a lot, look for ways to give him more physical exercise and mental challenge.

Pain

Your dog does not have words to tell you when something is wrong, but there are signs to look for to tell if your dog is in pain.

If your dog has been injured or is sick, you may notice that they favor a paw or do not want to be touched in a particular place. You might notice excessive licking. Or your dog might withdraw and seem depressed.

Chronic pain, such as an older dog will experience with arthritis, starts slowly and builds over time. You will notice symptoms such as stiffness, difficulty jumping or climbing stairs.

As they say with parents and children, you know your dog the best. If your dog is not acting like her normal self, she may be telling you that she does not feel well and is in pain. Consult with your vet for the best strategy to diagnose the cause and relieve the pain.

VOCALIZATION

So far as we know, human beings are the only animals that use language, that is, words or symbolic sounds that are combined to express simple thoughts and complex ideas. But many animals, including dogs, do use sound to communicate things to each other about the world.

Dogs make a lot of different sounds. They bark, growl, whine, howl, yelp, and yip. Based on context, each sound has a different meaning.

Some sounds dogs make are high-pitched, others low. We understand that a low pitched sound is more aggressive. This is because larger animals generally make lower pitched sounds.

Here's what the sounds your dog makes might mean.

Barking, Yelping, and Yipping

If you ask a child what sound a dog makes, they are likely to bark themselves or go, "Bow-wow." Barking says "dog" to us.

Except for the Basenji, all dogs bark, although some dogs bark more than others.

There is a lot of variation in the basic bark, indicating the range of what barking can say. The meaning of a bark varies based on volume, pitch, the number of barks and the amount of time between barks.

- A series of low-pitched rapid barks is aggressive.
- A short, high-pitched bark, what we call a yip, might mean surprise.
- A more l0w-pitched sudden sound, a yelp, indicates pain.

There are lots of reasons that dogs bark. They might be saying, 'Look, a squirrel!' 'It is the mailman,' 'There is someone at the door,' or 'Pay attention to me!'

Barks are loud. Depending on the size of your dog, barking starts at about 70 decibels, which is the same as a shout, and can be as loud as 130 decibels, which is the same as a jet take-off or car horn (Garvey et al., 2016). As a result, barking can be annoying, especially if you have a dog who barks a lot.

But if you watch and listen to understand why your dog is barking, you can minimize this behavior.

For example, what if your dog is barking to get your attention? Is this something you want to encourage? If not, you can discourage the behavior by not giving in. Check to be sure there is no problem. If there is not, do not engage with the dog. Ignoring the attention-getting bark (while it can be difficult) is the best way to discourage the behavior. Think of it like letting your young child cry when they simply do not want to go to bed, instead of walking up and down the stairs to ask what's wrong.

At other times, your dog may bark with excitement, like when you are getting ready for a walk. Again, you can discourage the behavior by ignoring it. Simply be still and ignore your dog until the barking stops.

Some dogs bark when you go out and leave them alone. Usually, the dog will bark a couple of times, wait to see if you respond, then try again. If you are calm when you leave the dog, and greet the dog calmly when you return, your dog will learn to settle and wait quietly when you are gone.

Some dogs bark from boredom or anxiety if they are left alone too long. This is not the dog's fault—and it can be annoying to the neighbors. It is up to you to find a solution. It may be leaving the dog with interesting toys, or perhaps hiring a dog walker.

It turns out people are pretty good at interpreting a dog's barks, even if they do not have a dog of their own. Researchers in Hungary tested how well people could interpret the meaning of different barks, and the results were much more accurate than would have happened simply by chance (Gibeault, 2017b).

Growling and Snarling

Growling and snarling are a warning, especially a low-pitched growling snarl. Pay attention to these sounds.

A low, sustained growl means stay away. Some dogs growl like this to protect something they like, perhaps a bone or a favorite toy.

A growl can also warn strangers to stay away. One time, my friend, Maria, was walking alone in the woods with her dog. The dog started growling loudly and then she noticed a stranger stepping out of the trees. Maria had often seen strangers in the woods, but this time she listened to her dog and quickly walked the other way.

Shorter growls might indicate anxiety or fear, or that your dog is getting over-excited. You may also hear growling during play, for example when you are using a tug toy or when your dog is playing with another dog.

Humans can not always hear fine distinctions between a dog's growls, but we can see signs of the difference in their body language. Watch the dog.

Is your dog's tail wagging when he growls while you are playing tug? That is a sign that it may be time to take a break before the dog gets too excited and out of control.

Do you hear growling when your dog is playing with another dog? If so, do both dogs look relaxed? Are they playing nicely and taking turns? If they are, do not worry, the dogs are just talking to each other.

Whining

Whining is usually a sound of desire or distress.

Young puppies whine when they want something. Older dogs do too. For example, your dog might whine if he needs to go outside. Or she might whine to let you know she needs help getting a ball that she can not reach under a chair.

My Max uses a whine like this. Max knows that he gets a chew treat each night after dinner; if I do not give him the treat as quickly as he would like, he lets me know with a whine.

Other reasons your dog might whine are if he is lonely; if he is feeling anxious or stressed, or simply to get your attention.

Whining can be a submissive sound that your dog uses to say 'you are the boss' or even 'I'm sorry.' You will hear this whine when the dog is in a submissive posture.

There is also an excited whine that some dogs make when they are anticipating something they like, perhaps when she sees you are ready to take her for a walk, or when he knows someone he likes is at the door.

However, if your dog is lying down and is whining for no reason that you can see, the dog may be in pain. If this happens, you should call the vet.

Sighing

A sigh is a deep exhale. Your dog can tell you two different things with a sigh.

A sigh is typically a sound of contentment. You will hear this when your dog lies down with eyes half-closed and her head on her paws.

Then there is the sigh of disappointment. You will hear him sigh like this with his eyes open and looking at you.

However, if you hear your dog sigh and also moan or groan, there could be something wrong and you may want a vet to check it out.

Howling

We tend to think of howling as something wolves do rather than dogs, but dogs can howl, too. Hounds, in particular, are dogs that will howl.

Among wolves, howling is a sound of distress or isolation, and a dog left alone too long might howl for this reason, too.

Howling is also a way to call out to other dogs, or to express territory. If you have more than one dog, if one dog starts to howl the others will join in.

Some people teach their dog to howl on cue, often by howling themselves. And some dogs spontaneously howl along when their humans are playing a musical instrument.

Baying

Baying, on the other hand, is a challenge. This is a deep, prolonged series of barks that your dog may make if there is an intruder. Dogs also bay when they are chasing something during a hunt.

TALKING JUST TO YOU

One of the great joys of owning a dog is the special bond you form and the way you and your dog come to understand each other.

Of course, it is different for everyone, but my dogs have had so much to tell me!

My Max always has something to say.

Jack Russell Terriers are well known for how they use their eyes to communicate. When Max wants some love or a cuddle, he will jump on the bed or couch, look directly into my eyes, and brush his paw against my arm. I will always scoot him closer to me and start to massage his shoulders and back.

When he feels like having a treat he will stand near the refrigerator, sit and look up at the bag of treats atop it. Then I will just ask him "Oh, did you want a treat?" and he will start to wag his tail so I know that is exactly what he wants.

If he ever wants more food or water he will sit in the kitchen and look at me. I know which he wants when I ask him "Do you want water?" or "Do you want food?" Whichever question he licks his lips to is what he wants. He makes it very easy.

There are other things he does to talk to me, too.

If he wants a potty break apart from his routine, he will stand by the door and scratch it one time. Then I will ask him, "Do you have to go potty?" Then he will stare at me, sit, and wait for me to get up to take him outside.

If he is cold at night, he will jump on the bed and scratch at my feet to let him under the covers. He knows it is warm under the blankets.

When he wants to play a bit in the house, he will get his ball, drop it on the floor in front of me, and then give a play bow, letting me know he wants to play and what he wants to play.

And when we have been outside for a bit and he is ready to come in and take a nap or relax, he will walk back to the door and sit next to it or place his paw on the door, making it clear that he is done and wants to go back inside.

I have heard so many amazing things from other people who have dogs, too.

I have a colleague, Barbara, whose daughter, Geri, is in college. Geri and her friends all love the family dog, an older Golden Retriever named Rose, and Geri likes to have Rose come for weekend visits.

Rose loves the visits, but she is getting up there in years and it really wears her out.

When Barbara drives Rose to the school it is the only time Rose wears a seat belt. And, starting after the first trip, every time Barbara puts Rose in the car and fastens the seat belt, Rose wiggles around with joy, then curls right up on the seat and is asleep within two blocks. Barbara knows what Rose is saying: 'This is going to be so fun! I had better rest up.'

Or another friend, Joe, has a Silken Windhound, Slim. These fast, silky hounds were bred from Whippets, Borzois, and Shelties; and they are built like clothes hangers. Joe wanted an activity to share with Slim. Even though Silken Windhounds are sighthounds rather than scenthounds, he decided to try Barn Hunting, a sport where dogs learn to hunt for rats. The rats are fine (they are protected in pipes that are hidden in the straw). The dogs sniff out the rats, and they are taught to point or paw at the straw where a rat is hidden.

Well, Slim was more subtle than that. When he got next to the rat, he'd simply pause briefly and look sideways at Joe. Joe would call for the find, and the other handlers could never believe it when Slim got it right.

8

HOW TO TALK TO YOUR DOG

Since dogs communicate largely through body language, everything you do will say something to your dog. But we also talk to our dogs through training.

This chapter is about training, because training is the formal language we use to let our dogs know what is good behavior and what we want them to do. It is the basis of positive communication between you and your dog.

Before we get into that, though, let's talk about simply the activities of daily life, which is the other important way we talk to our dogs.

From day one, you want your dog to get to know his name. Use his name all the time—when you are petting and playing with him, and when you are asking him to do something. When you introduce his name, start by having some treats in your hand. Call the dog's name, and give him a treat the moment he looks at you. Dogs like this!

This name calling activity is also a good way to teach your dog to pay attention to you whenever you call his name.

The easiest way to teach a dog how you want him to behave is to let him know what you expect from the start. For example, 'sit' is a common, and very useful command. You can certainly wait to teach the dog this by attending a puppy socialization or basic obedience class. But you can also teach the dog right from the start by asking him to sit before a pleasurable experience, such as before every meal and when you are putting on the leash to go for a walk.

An easy way to let your dog know what 'sit' means, is to hold a treat in front of the dog with one hand. Move your hand so the treat passes over the dogs head. As the dog looks up to follow the treat, use your other hand to gently push the dog's backside into the sit position. Do this before every meal, and your dog will quickly understand.

I also find it useful to teach the 'wait' command at mealtime and before a walk. I needed to use a leash the first few times with Max, who is very head-strong. With a puppy or small, quiet dog, a gentle hand in front of their face may be enough.

I had Max on the leash and put the leash on the floor under my foot so he couldn't lunge for the food bowl. I had him 'sit,' and then told him to 'wait.' Once Max was sitting patiently (or at least quietly), I took my foot off the leash and said 'okay.' At this point, Max dove for his dinner bowl! I no longer need the leash, but we still do this every night.

Especially if you have kids, one fun way to teach your dog to come when you call is also a good way to give the dog some exercise and socialization. Each person takes a handful of treats and stands a distance away from each other. One person is holding the dog. Then someone across the circle starts by holding out a treat and calling the dog to come. Everyone takes turns calling the dog by name and telling him to 'come.'

Once your dog understands what 'come' means, reinforce the command regularly. That way your dog will be more likely to listen when there is something else that competes for her attention.

The key is to make teaching your dog, talking to your dog, a normal part of everyday life.

I learned a useful tip from Cesar Millan about the best way to communicate with a dog. Millan says that you need to keep in mind first, that he is a dog. Second, that he is a particular breed of dog. And third, that he is an individual dog with his own personality.

I've certainly seen the truth of this when I think about the different dogs I have had. You may have noticed from the many breeds of dog that I have had in my life, I like a dog with a mind of his own. All of my dogs—Jack Russell Terrier, Chow Chow, Doberman, Rottweiler, and Miniature Pinscher—are prone to taking charge if you let them. Even a Chihuahua can be feisty and aggressive if not well socialized.

But each of my dogs was quite different, even Jack and Max, my Jack Russell Terriers. Once I understood the fundamental nature of the breed, good communication meant that I also needed to appreciate the personality of each dog. So I use knowing about dogs and breeds of dogs to guide the tools, the methods, I use to communicate with Max. I use what I know about Max to guide how I use those tools.

THE PACK MENTALITY

I've always heard that dogs are pack animals, living naturally in packs where one dog is dominant and the others submissive.

We can not know for sure what the dynamic was for the proto-wolf that became today's dog. But it seems likely that wild dogs lived and hunted together before forming a partnership with humans. Both behaviors require cooperation and leadership.

What I do know is that a pack is a social group, and a dog is a very social animal. Domestication, then, selected for dogs that want to be with us.

We talked earlier about a dog's brain being equivalent to that of a two or three year-old child. This does not mean that dogs never grow up. It means that your dog, like a young child, is comforted by structure, routine, and confident leadership.

A dog will look for a natural leader. That needs to be you.

Actions Speak Louder Than Words

How you behave around your dog will have an enormous influence on how your dog behaves. Consistency matters.

If your family has a dog and you want the dog to behave in a certain way, everyone in the family needs to be on board. If one person lets the dog sit on the sofa, or one person feeds the dog from the table, the dog will think these things are okay. She may know that sitting on the sofa is not okay with you, but if the children do not enforce the rule too, you will come home to find the dog on the sofa with them.

Be careful about roughhousing. You might enjoy wrestling with the dog in play. But be aware that you will be teaching your dog behavior that can be dangerous around young children. If the dog wrestles with you, he will think wrestling is okay with other people.

How you behave when you are taking your dog for a walk also says a lot, too. You will be walking together for your dog's entire life and you want it to be a pleasurable experience for both of you.

For us, we want our dogs to behave nicely on the lead—no tugging, biting the leash, dawdling, or jerking you around. You have to nip these behaviors in the bud, right from day one. Because, if you let your dog do something once it will take a long time to teach her that it really is not okay.

If you want your dog to walk with you nicely, make sure the dog is calm before you put her on the leash. You should be the one to go out the door first. Keep the dog near you. You decide when the dog can stop to sniff around.

Energy

Have you ever found yourself sitting somewhere, perhaps reading a book at the library or talking with a friend at a party, and realized that someone is looking at you? You can feel their gaze. Cesar Millan calls this the universal language of energy and emotion—one that dogs and other animals speak much more fluently than we humans (Millan & Peltier, 2006).

I do not know if it is energy or simply the fact that our dogs can perceive things that we cannot—notice movement that is inconspicuous to us, hear things we can not hear, and especially smell things that are imperceptible to us. But the dynamic is real.

Dogs understand our emotional states. If you are happy, sad, calm, excited, or nervous, your dog will know. That awareness affects how your dog reacts to you.

When you are talking to your dog, projecting a feeling of calm authority is the best way to get her to listen to you.

Watch what happens, for example, when a dog who knows the meaning of the word 'sit' is told to sit by you or by an excited child. You know your dog knows how to sit, and you project this when you give the command. The child, on the other hand, is thrilled to think that he can get the dog to do a trick. He is probably wiggling around, speaking in a high, excited voice, saying "Sit! Sit! Sit!" The dog may hear the word sit, but what she sees is an invitation to play.

Training

There are many different training techniques. I do not want to tell you how to train your dog. Some dogs work particularly well with one technique or another. Some people find it easier to use one technique or another. You will want to use the method(s) that are right for you and your dog.

Different training books and websites will give you different guidance about how often to train your dog. Some training does require a serious time commitment, but for the typical household pet I do not think you need a formal training session of 30 or even 15 minutes a day. I think incorporating training into daily life is the way to go.

The goal is a combination of teaching new behaviors, and interrupting and correcting bad behaviors.

Here are some general training tips that I have found very helpful.

Positive Reinforcement

We know today that positive reinforcement is the most effective way to train your dog. In other words, praise the behaviors you like and ignore—do not punish—the behaviors you do not want.

Motivate your dog with the rewards that are of highest value to him.

Reprimand Without Punishment

Try to discourage behavior you do not want by ignoring it. This is because to a dog, your attention can be a reward. When you need to reprimand your dog, use a sharp "No!" or a loud noise the dog does not like rather than physical punishment. Use your authoritative energy when you do this. If you are laughing when you tell the dog no, she won't believe you.

Sometimes a non-punitive training aid can be helpful. I do not mean a shock collar or anything like that. Rather, using something that makes a loud noise that the dog does not like, such as a can of pebbles or pennies, can be an effective way to get your message across.

I found that Max really does not like the aerosol sound of something called Pet Corrector. It only took two squirts of noise to teach him that he shouldn't attack the mail when it came through the slot.

Timing Matters

Timing is how your dog understands the connection between her behavior and a consequence. Feedback after the fact is meaningless to a dog when you can not use your words to explain what you are doing and why.

Be Consistent

Consistency is how you help your dog develop good habits.

Use Hand Signals

Using hand signals together with voice commands will let you talk to your dog over long distances.

Hand signals can also be very helpful if your dog suffers from hearing loss as she gets older.

Do Not Overtrain

If you overtrain, your dog can get bored. He may also become less likely to think for himself and make good choices.

Different dogs will learn more or less quickly, but even for a stubborn dog like a Jack Russell Terrier, a couple of repetitions of a command, perhaps twice a day, will be enough. And this is even easier if you incorporate the commands into what you do every day.

SOCIALIZATION

Socialization is one of the most important things you can do to train your dog, because the more your dog experiences, the better the dog will handle what comes her way later in life. Do your best to make sure she encounters all kinds of people, all kinds of other dogs, and all kinds of places.

Socialization starts with the bond between a puppy, mother dog, and littermates. If your dog was not well socialized as a puppy, you may need to teach him how to play nicely, without nipping, body slamming, or dominating the play. When you start to teach your dog to play, have him on a leash. Call your dog away when you see that things are getting too rough. The other dog may try to teach your dog good behavior, but when dogs are older this kind of communication can result in injuries that puppies do not give each other.

You will recognize well-socialized play when you see the dogs giving each other appeasement signals such as play bows, sneezing, yawning or licking. Watch to be sure each dog is responding to them.

You also want to make sure to introduce your dog to as many different types of people and places as you can. This will help him be confident, whatever the future brings.

WORKING WITH A PUPPY

Puppies need a lot of your time. They do sleep a lot, but when they are awake it can seem like they need to go to the bathroom every hour—or more. And their natural curiosity and canine way of exploring the world can be hazardous to your house.

The best method of housetraining is to avoid accidents. Keep the puppy in a crate when you are not around. Dogs do not like to soil where they sleep and, as long as you do not leave the puppy in the crate too long, she will not soil in there.

When he is out of the crate, watch your puppy for signs he needs to pee and take him outside before he goes to the bathroom on the rug. If your puppy can not yet sleep through the night you may need to set your alarm to take him out once or twice during the night.

Teaching commands to your new puppy can be easier than training an older dog, but only if you are able to ignore how cute she is! It will be much harder to break your teenage or adult dog of a bad habit if, when she was a puppy, you simply laughed when she gnawed on your hand, jumped up on you, or nibbled at your shoe.

Touch your young dog often, but gently.

It is also important to teach puppies and young dogs that it is okay when a human hand reaches toward them. Reach out slowly, let the puppy sniff, and then give him a rub.

Some breeders even start training puppies before sending them to their new homes. My friend Susan's new puppy already knew how to sit and come when

Susan got her at seven weeks old. Susan still needed to reinforce the commands (puppies can forget just like children do). But that early training was a great start.

BASIC COMMANDS FOR EVERYDAY LIFE

You may not like the idea of training, and you may not want to teach your dog tricks. But the fact is, everything you do teaches your dog something. And there are some basic commands that you should teach them that will make your life together much more pleasant.

It helps if you do not consider these commands 'tricks.' Instead, think of them as what your dog needs to know in order to live happily and safely in a human world.

Also, when you are working with the commands, be careful to give a command only once. If you get in the habit of saying "Sit. Sit. Sit." or "Come. Come on, boy. Come," your dog will think that those are the actual commands.

Here are ten things your dog needs to know, and it is easy to make learning them a fun part of daily life.

1. *Sit*

I learned to use the opportunity of daily meals and walks to teach my dogs to sit. Dogs will learn quickly when the reward is something they really want!

'Sit' is a particularly useful command because it can accomplish so many things. Do you want your dog to stop jumping up on you? Tell her to sit. Want your dog to stop running around? Tell her to sit. The unwanted behavior stops with the dog doing something positive rather than you yelling at them.

1. *Leave It*

Your dog explores the world with his nose and mouth, and there are lots of things you do not want him to eat or chew.

'Leave It' is a command to use before your dog has something in his mouth.

You start to teach 'Leave It' indoors in a controlled situation. The first step is for your dog to associate the words "leave it" with the action. To create this association, hold a treat in your hand. The dog will sniff and try to get it. As soon as the dog starts to move his mouth away, say "leave it" and tell him "good boy." Only give him the treat when he stops reaching for it.

Next, put a few treats on the floor. With the dog on leash, walk toward the treats. As soon as you see the dog look toward or start to reach for the treats say "Leave it" and hold the leash firmly while you walk by. Gradually introduce other objects, perhaps a young child's toy or something enticing from the trash and start including this command when you see something you do not want your dog to put in his mouth during your walks out of doors.

1. *Drop It*

'Drop It' is a related and equally useful command.

You teach 'Drop It' when the dog already has something in his mouth.

Your training starts using what's called a high value treat—something the dog really likes—combined with a relatively low value toy. While your dog is holding the toy in her mouth, offer her the treat. If she wants the treat enough, she will drop the toy to get the treat. As the toy drops from her mouth, say "drop it," praise her, and give her the treat.

Once this behavior is reliable, slowly start to give the command using praise with less desirable treats until, ultimately, you are using praise alone.

Teaching the 'Drop It' command will encourage your dog to be less possessive. It will be very useful if you ever see your dog put something dangerous in her mouth.

'Drop It' is also an important command if you and your dog like to play tug.

Most dogs love to play tug. There was a time that we were told that playing tug would make a dog aggressive; but research now shows that it can be a healthy activity (Nicholas, 2020).

However, you need your dog to learn to play tug by the rules. There are only three: 1) you are the one who starts the game, 2) the dog should not touch you with his mouth, and 3) the command 'Drop It' must be obeyed.

If your dog does not follow the rules, stop the play.

1. *Wait*

'Wait' is both good manners and a safety command.

It can mean 'do not dash out into traffic' or 'do not run out the door just because it is open.'

I started teaching 'Wait' to Max when I was giving him a meal. I also tell him to 'Wait' before we walk out the door.

It is easy to teach a small puppy to wait with a gentle restraining hand. With larger or older dogs, you will need to use a leash. Simply tell the dog to 'Wait' and prevent her from moving.

You can use the command to teach your dog to halt beside you when you cross the street. Some dogs will even learn to look both ways before crossing simply by observing you.

If you have a strong dog, you can use the wait command to teach your dog to walk quietly beside you when you go down stairs. To do this, simply stop at the top of the steps and tell the dog 'Wait.' When the dog is still, say 'Easy' and start down the steps. The moment the dog starts to move ahead, stop and say 'Wait.'

At first you are likely to stop at every step. Very soon, the dog will walk easily beside you all the way down.

1. *Come*

Everyone wants a dog who will come when she is called.

If your new dog is a puppy, take advantage of the fact that the puppy wants to be with you (I call it the duckling instinct). When you turn away, the puppy will naturally follow, so be sure to tell him to 'Come.' However, while this is a great start, you will need to continue the training for a long time, most challengingly through the dog's teenage years.

Just like human teens, teenage dogs will test the limits of the rules. It will probably seem that you are having to teach the dog to come all over again.

This is a great time to use the 'Come, Come, Come' game that I used to teach Max (the game where everyone gets in a circle, calls the dog to them, and gives him a treat when he reaches them).

Another way to teach your dog to come is to use the command to bring your dog to your side before a meal (of course, this only works if your dog is not sitting there eagerly already).

Many trainers recommend that you start to teach the 'Come' command in a low-distraction indoor environment before trying it outside because 'Come' can be a challenging command for your dog when he is outside, off-leash, and having a wonderful time.

When you are teaching 'Come,' it is also important to make sure the dog actually comes all the way to you. Do not let her get away with just getting close.

I mentioned earlier that you should combine verbal commands with hand signals, and this can be especially useful when teaching 'Come,' because your dog will often be far away when you use it.

1. *Off*

This is a command that will keep your dog away from kitchen counters and off of the table.

The Pet Corrector aerosol spray can be a great tool to use when teaching this command. This is because 'Off' is a correction to stop an existing behavior, not a command to teach a new behavior; so you need to catch the culprit in the act, and you may be across the room.

When you see your dog start to jump up to sniff at the counter, give a spritz and say 'Off.' When you are sitting at the table, a simple push away should do the trick.

Of course, the best way to keep the dog off is to never, never feed the dog from the counter or the table. You may want to give your dog table scraps, and that is fine, but never feed the dog scraps from the counter or while you are sitting at the table. When you are done, scrape the plates into the dog's food bowl, and only give the scraps to your dog then.

1. ***Do Not Bite***

This is a behavior rather than a command.

Ideally your dog will have learned at least the rudiments of 'Do Not Bite' during their first three to eight weeks of play with his littermates. You will need to reinforce this so the dog understands he needs to be even more gentle with those fragile humans and their thin skin.

If your dog puts her open mouth on you, do not pull away or slap at her. Instead, freeze. Turn your attention away. When the dog removes her mouth, turn back to her and give her affection. It is natural for her to use her mouth like we would use our hands, and she does not understand that it hurts.

Puppies, as you probably know, have tiny needle teeth that can really hurt. The puppy is not trying to hurt you. If your puppy uses her teeth on you during play, give her a toy to put in her mouth instead.

However, if your puppy continues to use her teeth to play rough with you, you should immediately withdraw from the play. What might be considered painful but cute in a puppy can be dangerous in an adult dog.

1. *Settle*

I first learned about this command when I was Googling the internet to find out what commands service puppy raisers teach their dogs, and I became an immediate convert.

The 'Settle' command means 'calm down, be still, and entertain yourself.'

To teach your dog to settle, put on the leash and walk with the dog to your desk or a chair where you plan to sit for a while. While the dog is sitting or standing near you, put the leash on the ground and put your foot on the leash so the dog can not move away but has enough room to sit or lie down comfortably. Tell the dog 'Settle,' and go about your business.

By keeping your foot on the leash, you will prevent the dog from moving away. If your dog barks, whines, or pulls, ignore him. Simply continue with what you are doing.

At first the dog won't stay quiet for very long. That is okay. What you want to do is start slowly. At first, release the dog as soon as she has settled quietly for a little while. Then, gradually increase the amount of time your dog can quietly wait by your side.

As an added bonus, once your dog understands the command to 'Settle,' you can use it to help him calm down if he is feeling a little wild.

1. *Walking Nicely on Lead*

I have heard it said that, in order to teach your dog to walk nicely on a lead, you should never let your dog walk in front because being in front means the dog thinks he is in charge. I do not agree.

Being in front does not necessarily mean being in charge. Being in charge means being in control.

For your dog, daily walks are more than simply an opportunity to relieve herself. Walks are opportunities to experience the outside world. This is why I do not subscribe to the idea that you should never let your dog be in front on a walk.

Yes, good leash behavior includes not tugging or biting the lead. But I also want to let my dog experience the world with all his senses. This means a lot of sniffing (which tells him a lot that I simply do not understand). Sometimes he will want to follow a scent ahead of me. Sometimes he wants to turn around to follow a scent back for a while before continuing on. As long as he is not tugging or pulling, that is okay with me.

So I've taught Max a couple of things. "Sidewalk" means 'stay on this side of the road.' "Back Around" means 'I see you wrapped your leash around that bush, so it is up to you to unwrap it.' "Let's Go" means 'time to move on.'

So at times Max walks beside me, sometimes in back, and sometimes in front. It works for us.

Up and over I go!

FORMAL OBEDIENCE TRAINING

Beyond the training needed to socialize and accustom your dog to behaving well in everyday life, there are many opportunities to get involved in more extensive training and other dog activities. Let's take a look.

There are two major breed clubs in the U.S. The larger of the two is the non-profit American Kennel Club (AKC). The other club is the for-profit United Kennel Club (UKC).

AKC and UKC have their own breed standards. AKC registers only U.S. breeds and UKC includes international breeds, but both keep pedigree records for dogs registered to their standards. Both clubs also sponsor conformation shows and offer formal training programs with obedience and performance-based activities. There are events for juniors as well as adults.

Family Dog Programs

These are classes that focus on the basic training a dog needs to become what AKC calls a "Canine Good Citizen" (CGC).

AKC offers four levels of programs focused on teaching a family dog. These classes start with S.T.A.R. Puppy, open to vaccinated puppies up to a year old. Young puppies learn to sit and lie down, walk on leash, tolerate the kind of handling they will experience on trips to the vet, and demonstrate socialization behaviors such as allowing their person to take a toy out of their mouth.

After S.T.AR. puppy, there is the CGC class, which focuses on good manners. AKC Community Canine expands the training to typical real-life situations such as teaching the dog to wait while you are doing something and allow a stranger to approach. Urban CGC is a similar course designed specifically for dogs who live in the city.

UKC also has classes for puppies aged three to six months. These classes are focused on elementary obedience commands.

Taking a training class like one of these is a good idea, even if you are confident of your ability to teach good manners to your dog. This is because the classes are a good socialization opportunity.

Novice, Open, & Utility Obedience

Obedience classes are the traditional training that start with basic commands such as sit, down, and stay.

AKC offers Novice, Open, and Utility obedience classes. Once the dog/handler team has mastered basic commands at the Novice level, they can advance to Open. In Open, dogs and their handlers work off-leash and learn basic retrieving and jumping. At the next level, Utility, the skills include scent work and silent signaling activities.

The UKC has similar Basic and Advanced obedience training programs.

Conformation Dog Shows

Conformation shows, like the televised Westminster Kennel Club and National Dog Shows, are often called the beauty contests of the canine world. Dogs are judged by appearance and demeanor by breed, each compared to the club's breed standard.

Conformation shows are the only events that are open exclusively to purebred dogs.

In order to compete in Conformation your dog will need obedience training as well as to get acclimated to being touched by show judges during the event.

Many breeds also have special grooming needs for conformation. The Havanese is a good example of this. A Havanese dog that competes in conformation has long hair that reaches the ground. Most Havanese family pets, on the other hand, have a short clip that is much easier to care for.

One thing I learned about what you see on these shows concerns how the dog handlers use the leash.

In conformation shows the leash is placed high on the dog's neck. When I first saw this, I thought it could choke the dog, but the dogs in the shows look like they are having a good time.

The dog is aware of the leash placed this way. It is snug, but the leash is not tight.

It turns out the reason to use high-neck leash place-ment is to give you the best control, which actually avoids the problem of having to constantly pull at the dog's neck when they are learning to walk on lead.

I learned this from a friend who was having a hard time controlling her boisterous Sheepadoodle, Rex. The trainer told her about high-neck leash placement, and Rex stopped pulling right away.

CANINE SPORTS AND ACTIVITIES

If you have the time and interest, there are a host of other activities you can do with your dog. These include companion sports—things you and your dog do together—and performance sports—activities that were created based on the abilities of different breed groups: hounds, terriers, retrievers, herders, pointers, and spaniels. Here are a few. This is by no means a comprehensive list, but it will give you an idea of the range of activities you might find in your area.

Companion Sports

Tricks

Want to have some fun with your dog? Take this class to learn tricks like how to crawl, get in a box, shake hands, give a high five, jump through a hoop, put paws up on a step, do a push up, and spin & twist. Maybe he can even star in his own videos or win a talent show on TV!

Agility

Agility is a kind of canine gymnastics. Dogs race through an obstacle course one at a time. The winner is the dog who negotiates the course fastest and with the fewest mistakes. Your dog will learn to jump and climb, run through tunnels, cross raised walkways, and negotiate weave poles. The goal is to get through the course cleanly in the least amount of time. This is a great activity for a high energy dog.

Rally

Rally is a sport that is based on obedience training. You and your dog will negotiate a course with as many as 20 signs. Each sign instructs you to perform a specific skill. Speed is not a factor here. The winner is the dog/handler team that performs the most tricks correctly and with the best teamwork and enjoyment. This sport can be fun for dogs of all energy levels.

Free Style

Free Style is an activity for people who like to dance. You will create a routine of tricks to do with your dog, choreographed to music. You and your dog learn the routine and then compete with other dog/handler teams at Free Style shows. Dogs aren't really known for their sense of rhythm, so getting your dog to move in sync with you is one of the challenges of Free Style.

One of the most amazing Free Style performances I have ever seen is a military routine that tied for first place at Crufts, the British International Dog Show, in 2017. This routine does not have as much dancing as is typical; instead the dog and handler do a kind of a play and the dog even does CPR (Deril And Lusy - Canine Freestyle - Crufts 2017, 2021). You can find the video posted on several websites.

Flyball

Flyball is a team competition. A group of four dogs forms a relay. Each dog races over a 51-foot course with four hurdles. At the far end of the course, the dog presses on a box to release a tennis ball, which the dog catches, and then holds the ball in her mouth while she races back down the hurdle course. The four dogs go in turn. The winning team is the one that finishes fastest with the fewest errors (dropped balls, missed hurdles, or early starts).

Frisbee

I have often seen folks out with their dogs playing frisbee, sometimes with the human plastic kind and sometimes with a softer disc. There is also a sport called Disc Dog where you can compete in either distance throwing or freestyle.

Performance Sports

Dock Jumping

Dock Jumping, which is also called Dock Diving, is an event for dogs who like to swim and play fetch. The sport is simple. You stand on a dock and toss a toy into the water. The dogs compete to see who goes the highest and farthest when jumping off the dock to retrieve the toy. This is a relatively new sport

Lure Coursing

Sighthounds love to chase things, and Lure Coursing is a sport designed for sighthounds, although any dog can play. The sport uses a mechanical lure that is attached to a pulley. The course is 600 or more feet long, and the lure is pulled in a zig-zag fashion for the dogs to chase. You can either do Tests or Trials. Tests are simply recreational. Trials are competitions where dogs run in groups of three and are judged based on things like speed, agility, and endurance. Lure Coursing is about the chase.

Weight Pull

Weight Pull is a sport based on freighting, which is one of the jobs that strong dogs used to do, pulling loaded carts. In the modern sport dogs might pull either a weighted cart or a sled. This tends to be a game that the bully breeds like, which is a good thing because there are so many bully mix dogs these days.

Herding

This is a natural activity for the Herding breeds, but many dogs can learn the commands. You may have heard some of them: 'Come by,' 'Away to me,' 'Get out,' 'That'll do.' They are redolent of the days when most herding dogs were trained to do what they do best. The challenge with this activity is finding somewhere to train and practice, not to mention livestock to herd.

One way trained herding dogs are used today is for the Geese Police, dogs who scare Canada Geese away in suburban locations.

SPECIALTY TRAINING

Service Dogs

You may have seen one—an adorable puppy wearing a blue and yellow cape following her person into the office. This is a service dog in training.

Prospective service puppies learn from the very start how to behave well in all situations. Dog enthusiasts volunteer to raise the young puppies and give them the basic training they need in order to learn to assist someone with a disability. The dogs then undergo many months of additional training before being paired with a human handler.

Seeing Eye Dogs are the most common type of service dog. But dogs are also trained as Hearing Dogs, Wheelchair Assistance Dogs, and to help people with health issues like diabetes, seizures, autism, or PTSD.

Service dogs are allowed by law to go everywhere with their handler, and so the socialization and training requirements are extensive.

Therapy Dogs

Therapy dogs also require training and require certification to go into public places, but the training is not nearly as extensive as needed for service dogs. Therapy dogs must know the basic commands included in AKC's Canine Good Citizen, and must demonstrate the right personality. There are therapy dog classes available in most communities.

Dogs who might make good therapy dogs are dogs who are calm and enjoy meeting lots of people.

Therapy dogs go with their handlers to visit people who are in nursing homes, hospitals, libraries, or schools. Therapy dogs also go to disaster sites to help comfort victims there.

Search and Rescue

Search and Rescue dogs are trained to find people by scent. They work in law enforcement, the military, and volunteer with the Red Cross for disaster relief.

These dogs have found people in all environments from the wilderness to the city. Think of the famous image of the St. Bernard, barrel of brandy around his neck, who goes out to find someone buried by an avalanche. Or the amazing teams of dogs and handlers who worked so hard at the World Trade Center after 9/11.

If your dog is trained in Search & Rescue, you can participate in Tracking events that are based on the same skills and that provide experience for dog and handler.

Dogs chose us.

Back in prehistoric times, a few curious wolves came into human settlements and thought, "I have a good thing here." And those early humans thought, "This could be a good thing for us, too."

I'm so glad, because there is something magic about having a dog in your life.

Living with, getting to know a dog, is special.

Dogs give us loyalty, companionship, and unconditional love. They do work for us. They entertain us. They get us up off our feet and out into the world, helping us to be healthier and less stressed.

And one of the most fascinating parts of the experience is getting to know the mind of your dog.

Every dog is a dog; and every dog is an individual, too. Through a respect for your new companion's basic dog-ness, careful observation, learning to know your dog's body language and vocalizations, and teaching your dog the basics of how to live happily in the human world, you and your dog will come to understand each other.

It takes consistency, confidence and a little time—but you do not need to invest in weeks or months of training classes. You can teach your dog what they need to know by making good behavior a part of your dog's everyday life—and it is worth every minute.

Once you understand a dog's basic nature and how their mind works, getting to know your pup's personality and how they express themselves is a wonderful experience.

And if you want to take it further, there are plenty of options for you and your pup to explore.

Aside from everything you've discovered and learned in this book, a few things to keep in mind and do your best in remembering is that, your pup is only with you for a short amount of time. Love them, let them love you, play with them, enjoy your walks around the neighborhood or time spent at the dog park. Take them with you to as many places or events as you're able too. A dog will always be there for you rain or shine without question, bias or any form of judgment. One, five, or ten+ years will come and go in a blink of an eye, so cherish and adore them while they're here, by your side. I personally believe dog's and humans were meant to meet and sync in this world, to be there for one another and to take on life together.

REFERENCES

AKC Staff. (2014, August 28). *How the sounds dogs make reveal their emotions.* American Kennel Club. https://www.akc.org/expert-advice/lifestyle/how-the-sounds-dogs-make-reveal-their-emotions/#:~:text=The%20most%20common%20-sounds%20of

American Kennel Club. (2022). American Kennel Club. https://www.akc.org/

AVMA Staff. (n.d.). *Canine tail docking FAQ.* American Veterinary Medical Association. https://www.avma.org/about/canine-tail-docking.aspx/canine-tail-docking-faq

Anderson, T. (n.d.). *5 reasons your dog is whining—and how to make him stop.* Modern Dog Magazine.

https://moderndogmagazine.com/articles/5-reasons-your-dog-whining-and-how-make-him-stop/114249

Baker, H. (2021, April 14). *Pet dog buried 6,000 years ago is earliest evidence of its domestication in Arabia.* Livescience.com. https://www.livescience.com/earliest-evidence-dog-domestication-arabian-peninsula.html

Barnes, R. (2019, July 8). *Understanding how dogs learn: the basics of learning theory.* Pawgress. https://www.pawgress.dog/post/understanding-how-dogs-learn-the-basics-of-learning-theory

Bekoff, M. (2000). Animal emotions: exploring passionate natures. *BioScience, 50(10), 861.* https://doi.org/10.1641/0006-3568(2000)050[0861:aeepn]2.0.co;2

Berns, G. (2020, April 15). *Decoding the canine mind.* Dana Foundation. https://dana.org/article/decoding-the-canine-mind/

Bradshaw, J. (2011). *Dog sense : How the new science of dog behavior can make you a better friend to your pet.* Basic Books.

Buzhardt, L. (2009). *How dogs use smell to perceive the world.* VCA Animal Hospitals. https://vcahospitals.-

com/know-your-pet/how-dogs-use-smell-to-perceive-the-world

Cartoons from the November 15, 2021, Issue. (2021, November 8). The New Yorker; Condé Nast. https://www.newyorker.com/cartoons/issue-cartoons/cartoons-from-the-november-15-2021-issue

Coren, S. (2008, November 5). *Building a better brain for your dog.* Psychology Today. https://www.psychologytoday.com/us/blog/canine-corner/200811/building-better-brain-your-dog

Coren, S. (2011a, April 19). *How good is your dog's sense of taste?* Psychology Today. https://www.psychologytoday.com/us/blog/canine-corner/201104/how-good-is-your-dogs-sense-taste

Coren, S. (2011b, November 11). *Do dogs feel jealousy and envy?* Psychology Today. https://www.psychologytoday.com/us/blog/canine-corner/201111/do-dogs-feel-jealousy-and-envy#:~:text=It%20is%20well%20accepted%20that

Coren, S. (2013). *Which emotions do dogs actually experience?* Psychology Today. https://www.psychologytoday.com/us/blog/canine-corner/201303/which-emotions-do-dogs-actually-experience

Coren, S. (2017, December 28). *Do dogs think about and plan for the future?* Psychology Today. https://www.psychologytoday.com/us/blog/canine-corner/201712/do-dogs-think-about-and-plan-the-future

Coren, S. (2021, July 29). *Do dogs really feel guilt? An informal demonstration.* Psychology Today. https://www.psychglogytoday.com/us/blog/canine-corner/202107/do-dogs-really-feel-guilt-informal-demonstration

Cosgrove, N. (2021, May 11). 25 *Most popular dog breeds in 2022 (with pictures & breed info).* Hepper. https://www.hepper.com/most-popular-dog-breeds/

Courtright, I. (n.d.). *Working dogs vs companion dogs: What's the difference?* Keen Dog Training. https://keendogtraining.com/working-dogs-vs-companion-dogs-difference/#:~:text=A%20work-ing%20dog%20is%20trained

DeCesare, L. (2020, January 30). *Why dogs want to be close to you.* Wag Walking. https://wagwalking.-com/behavior/why-dogs-want-to-be-close-to-you

Deril And Lusy - Canine Freestyle - Crufts 2017. (2021). Flixxy. https://www.flixxy.com/deril-and-lusy-canine-freestyle-crufts-2017.htm

Different types of working dogs – do you know the difference? (2020, September 25). Clovernook Center for the Blind and Visually Impaired. https://clovernook.org/2020/09/25/different-types-of-working-dogs-do-you-know-the-difference/

Dog & puppy classical conditioning training. (n.d.). Canine Scholars Dog Training. https://www.caninescholars.com/learning-principles/classical-conditioning/#:~:text=Classical%20

conditioning%20refers%20to%20a

Dog communication and body language. (2022). Center for Shelter Dogs. https://centerforshelterdogs.tufts.edu/dog-behavior/dog-communication-and-body-language/#:~:text=The%20difference%20is%2C%20while%20humans

Dog groups. (n.d.). Dog Time. https://dogtime.com/dog-breeds/groups#:~:text=Hound%20Dogs

Dogs sense of touch. (2021, March 9). Small Dog Place. https://www.smalldogplace.com/dogs-sense-of-touch.html

estaff. (2018, February 9). *Would your dog be happier with a second dog?* TuftsYourDog. https://www.tuftsyourdog.com/dogownership/would-your-dog-be-happier-with-a-second-dog/

Fratt, K. (2020, November 23). *5 Myths about nature vs nurture in dogs: genetics vs environment!* www.k9ofmine.com. https://www.k9ofmine.com/dog-nature-vs-nurture/

Gannon, M. (2017, November 20). *8,000-Year-old rock art includes the world's oldest images of dogs.* Livescience. https://www.livescience.com/60982-oldest-images-of-dogs-on-leashes.html

Garber, M. (2012, May 14). Humanity's best friend: How dogs may have helped humans beat the Neanderthals. *The Atlantic.* https://www.theatlantic.com/technology/archive/2012/05/humanitys-best-friend-how-dogs-may-have-helped-humans-beat-the-neanderthals/257145/

Garvey, M., Stella, J., & Croney, C. (2016). *Auditory stress: Implications for kenneled dog welfare.* https://extension.purdue.edu/extmedia/VA/VA-18-W.pdf

Geier, E. (2017, February 16). *7 Simple steps to creating a room just for your dog.* rover.com. https://www.rover.com/blog/7-simple-steps-creating-room-just-dog/#:~:text=The%20room%20it-self&text=A%20dog%20zone%20doesn

Gibeault, S. (2017a, November 10). *How different breeds seek eye contact differently.* American Kennel Club. https://www.akc.org/expert-advice/life-style/different-breeds-seek-eye-contact-different-ly/#:~:text=Staring%20into%20your%20dog

Gibeault, S. (2017b, December 22). *Learning to speak dog – The meaning of your dog's barks.* American Kennel Club. https://www.akc.org/expert-advice/lifestyle/learn-speak-dog-meaning-dogs-barks/

Goldman, J. G. (2010, September 6). Man's new best friend? A forgotten Russian experiment in fox domestication. *Scientific American Blog Network.* https://blogs.scientificamerican.com/guest-blog/mans-new-best-friend-a-forgotten-russian-experiment-in-fox-domestication/

Hauser, W. (n.d.). *Can dogs get depressed?* ASPCA Pet Health Insurance. https://www.aspcapetinsurance.-com/resources/can-dogs-get-depressed/

Heimbuch, J. (n.d.). *7 Things your senior dog would like to tell you.* Old Dog Haven. https://old-doghaven.org/7-things-your-senior-dog-would-like-to-tell-you/

History of Companion Dogs. (n.d.). Janedogs.com. https://janedogs.com/history-of-companion-dogs/

Horowitz, A. (2016a). *Being a dog: Following the dog into a world of smell.* Scribner.

Horowitz, A., & Thomson, S. L. (2016). *Inside of a dog.* New York Simon & Schuster Books For Young Readers ©B.

Horwitz, D., & Landsberg, G. (n.d.). *Dog behavior problems aggression sibling rivalry diagnosis.* VCA Animal Hospitals. https://vcahospitals.com/know-your-pet/dog-behavior-problems-aggression-sibling-rivalry-diagnosis

How dogs learn. (n.d.). Doggie Residence. https://www.doggieresidence.com/dogs-learn-dog-psychology-learning-theory/

How long should a puppy be with its mother? (2020, October 28). Hospital Veterinari Glòries. https://www.hospitalveterinariglories.com/puppy-with-its-mother/?lang=en

How many hours does a dog sleep in a day? (n.d.). Pet MD. https://www.petmd.com/dog/general-health/how-many-hours-does-dog-sleep-day

How powerful is a dog's nose? (2020, July 23). Phoenix Vet Center. https://phoenixvetcenter.com/blog/214731-how-powerful-is-a-dogs-nose

Hunger for words: meet Stella, the world's first talking dog! (2021). Hunger for Words. https://www.hungerforwords.com/

Non-sporting group dogs. (2020, August 17). k9perfection. https://k9perfection.net/2020/08/17/non-sporting-group-dogs/

Katayama, M., Kubo, T., Yamakawa, T., Fujiwara, K., Nomoto, K., Ikeda, K., Mogi, K., Nagasawa, M., & Kikusui, T. (2019). Emotional contagion from humans to dogs is facilitated by duration of ownership. *Frontiers in Psychology, 10.* https://doi.org/10.3389/fpsyg.2019.01678

Katz, B. (2018, February 28). A sickly paleolithic pupper only survived because of human help. *Smithsonian Magazine.* https://www.smithsonianmag.com/smart-news/14000-year-old-puppy-may-have-been-cared-paleolithic-humans-180968282/

Kawczynska, C. (2019, October 7). *The truth behind "designer dogs" and dog breeding.* www.thewildest.com. https://www.thewildest.com/dog-lifestyle/truth-behind-designer-dogs-and-dog-breeding

Kawczynska, C. (2021, June). *Q&A with Temple Grandin*. The Bark. https://thebark.com/content/qa-temple-grandin

Keller, H. (1904). *The Project Gutenberg ebook of The World I Live In, by Helen Keller*. Gutenberg. https://www.gutenberg.org/files/27683/27683-h/27683-h.htm#Page_77

Konno, A., Romero, T., Inoue-Murayama, M., Saito, A., & Hasegawa, T. (2016). Dog breed differences in visual communication with humans. *PLOS ONE, 11(10)*, *e0164760*. https://doi.org/10.1371/journal.pone.0164760

Leigh, P. (2021, April 13). *Puppy socialization starts with the breeder: early neurological stimulation*. American Kennel Club. https://www.akc.org/expert-advice/dog-breeding/breeder-puppy-socialization-early-neurological-stimulation/

Lewis, S. K. (2010, October 28). The meaning of dog barks — NOVA. *PBS*. https://www.pbs.org/wgbh/nova/nature/meaning-dog-barks.html

London, K. (2021, June). *Noise sensitivity and pain in dogs*. The Bark. https://thebark.com/content/noise-sensitivity-and-pain-dogs

Lotz, K. (2016, August 22). *Litter lessons: What your dog learns from his littermates & mother.* I Heart Dogs. https://iheartdogs.com/litter-lessons-what-your-dog-learns-from-his-littermates-mother/

Lowry, E. (2021, March 8). *How dogs sense the world around them.* Raw Feeders' Kitchen. https://rawfeed-erskitchen.com/how-dogs-sense-the-world-around-them/

Maldarelli, C. (2014, February 21). Although pure-bred dogs can be best in show, are they worst in health? *Scientific American.* https://www.scientifi-camerican.com/article/although-purebred-dogs-can-be-best-in-show-are-they-worst-in-health/

Mark, D. (2021, March 9). *The 7 best dog breeds for someone who works all day.* Pet Helpful. https://pethelpful.com/dogs/dogs-for-someone-who-works

McReynolds, T. (2018, March 26). *Study: noise sensitivity in dogs could be a sign of serious pain.* American Animal Hospital Association. https://www.aa-ha.org/publications/newstat/articles/2018-03/study-noise-sensitivity-in-dogs-could-be-a-sign-of-serious-pain/#:~:text=A%20new%20s-tudy%20conducted%20by

Meadows, B. (2021a, February 18). *What is the herding dog group?* Dog Time. https://dogtime.com/reference/71397-what-is-the-herding-dog-group

Meadows, B. (2021b, March 2). *What is the working dog group?* Dog Time. https://dogtime.com/reference/71467-working-dog-group#:~:text=Among%20this%20group%20are%20also

Millan, C., & Peltier, M. J. (2006). *Cesar's way: The natural, everyday guide to understanding and correcting common dog problems* (First). Random House, Inc.

Mood, A. (2019, August 5). *Chaser the dog: Remember the "smartest dog in the world."* American Kennel Club. https://www.akc.org/expert-advice/news/remembering-chaser-the-smartest-dog-in-the-world/

Morell, V. (2015). From wolf to dog. *Scientific American, 313(1),* 60–67. https://doi.org/10.1038/scientificamerican0715-60

Nelson, J. (2017, August 7). *Fear aggression in dogs and how to help.* I Heart Dogs https://iheartdogs.com/fear-aggression-in-dogs-and-how-to-help/

Nicholas, J. (2020, July 31). *Playing tug of war without encouraging aggression in dogs.* Preventive Vet.

https://www.preventivevet.com/dogs/playing-tug-of-war-without-encouraging-aggression-in-dogs

Patent, D. H. (2014). *Super Sniffers: Dog Detectives on the Job.* Bloomsbury.

Prichard, A., Chhibber, R., Athanassiades, K., Spivak, M., & Berns, G. S. (2018). Fast neural learning in dogs: A multimodal sensory fMRI study. *Scientific Reports, 8(1).* https://doi.org/10.1038/s41598-018-32990-2

Reisen, J. (2019a, August 15). *How much sleep do puppies need? Here's how to make sure.* American Kennel Club. https://www.akc.org/expert-advice/health/how-much-do-puppies-sleep/#:~:text=Although%20puppies%20are%20lit-tle%20bundles

Reisen, J. (2019b, November 8). *Physical and mental signs that your dog is aging.* American Kennel Club. https://www.akc.org/expert-advice/health/physi-cal-mental-signs-dog-aging/

Ripley, K. (2019, January 18). *Dog whining: why do dogs whine?* American Kennel Club. https://www.akc.org/expert-advice/training/rea-sons-your-dog-is-whining/

Robins, M. (2019, November 21). *Why does my dog hump? Understanding humping or mounting behavior.* American Kennel Club. https://www.akc.org/expert-advice/training/why-is-my-dog-humping-or-mounting/

Ross, W. (2020, October 27). How Science is Revolutionizing the World of Dog Training. *Time.* https://time.com/5880219/science-of-dog-training/

Rueb, E. S., & Chokshi, N. (2019, September 26). Labradoodle creator says the breed is his life's regret. *The New York Times.* https://www.nytimes.com/2019/09/25/us/labradoodle-creator-regret.html#:~:text=The%20inventor%20of

%20the%20labradoodle

Sheep dog commands. (2021, January 21). Patch Puppy. https://patchpuppy.com/dog-training/sheep-dog-commands/

Siniscalchi, M., d'Ingeo, S., Minunno, M., & Quaranta, A. (2018). Communication in dogs. *Animals, 8(8), 131.* https://doi.org/10.3390/ani8080131

Soukiasian, K. A. (2016, November 13). *How your dog plays reveals her temperament and personality.* Dog's Best Life. https://dogsbestlife.com/home-page/dog-plays-reveals-temperment-personali-ty/#:~:text=Neutral%2C%20and%20Passive.-

Stages of puppy development. (2018, May 7). Dogtime. https://dogtime.com/puppies/1130-puppy-behav-ior-basics-hsus#/slide/1

Stilwell, V. (2016). *The secret language of dogs: Unlocking the canine mind for a happier pet* (First). Penguin Random House LLC.

The friend who keeps you young. (n.d.). Hopkins Medi-cine. https://www.hopkinsmedi-cine.org/health/wellness-and-prevention/the-friend-who-keeps-you-young

United Kennel Club. (2022). United Kennel Club. https://www.ukcdogs.com/home

Uvnäs-Moberg, K., Handlin, L., & Petersson, M. (2015). Self-soothing behaviors with particular reference to oxytocin release induced by non-noxious sensory stimulation. *Frontiers in Psychology, 5.* https://doi.org/10.3389/fpsyg.2014.01529

Vanacore, C. B. (2019). *Dog.* Encyclopædia Britan-nica. https://www.britannica.com/animal/dog

Viegas, J. (2012, February 10). *Dogs understand us better than chimps do.* Livescience. https://www.livescience.com/18411-dogs-understand-humans-chimps.html

Vieira de Castro, A. C., Fuchs, D., Morello, G. M., Pastur, S., de Sousa, L., & Olsson, I. A. S. (2020). Does training method matter? Evidence for the negative impact of aversive-based methods on companion dog welfare. *PLOS ONE, 15(12)*, *e0225023*. https://doi.org/10.1371/journal.pone.0225023

Walden, L. (2019, July 31). 8 Dog body language signs and the emotions they portray. *Country Living.* https://www.countryliving.-com/uk/wildlife/pets/a28407333/dog-body-language/

Waynick, L. (2021, September 24). *Why do dogs sigh?* The Spruce Pets. https://www.thesprucepets.-com/why-do-dogs-sigh-5199223

Weir, M., & Buzhardt, L. (2009). *Designer dog breeds.* VCA Animal Hospitals. https://vcahospitals.-com/know-your-pet/designer-dog-breeds

What is a sploot? We explain the frog legging doggy with the cutest pictures. (2018, May 8). Dog Buddy Blog. https://blog.dogbuddy.com/dog-news/hu-mour/what-is-a-sploot-explain-cutest-pictures/

What is temperament? (n.d.). American Kennel Club. https://www.akc.org/akctemptest/what-is-temperament/

Why is my dog whining? (2019, June 30). Cesar's Way. https://www.cesarsway.com/why-is-my-dog-whining/

Wilber, J. (2021, March 4). *10 Ideas for Spending Quality Time With Your Dog.* PetHelpful. https://pethelpful.com/dogs/Ten-Ideas-for-Spending-Quality-Time-with-Your-Dog

Wu, K. J. (2018, May 4). *You asked: How are pets different from wild animals?* Harvard University. https://sitn.hms.harvard.edu/flash/2018/asked-pets-different-wild-animals/

Zaraska, M. (2017, October 11). The sense of smell in humans is more powerful than we think. *Discover Magazine.* https://www.discovermagazine.com/mind/the-sense-of-smell-in-humans-is-more-powerful-than-we-think

Zug, G. R. (n.d.). *Jacobson's organ.* Encyclopædia Britannica. https://www.britannica.com/science/Jacobsons-organ

IMAGES

ArtHouse Studio. (2020 May 5). *Rocky formation with rough surface and painting.* Pexels. [Image]. https://www.pexels.com/photo/rocky-formation-with-rough-surface-and-painting-4328432/

Comfreak. (n.d.) *Dog puppy young dog.* Pixabay. [Image]. https://pixabay.com/photos/dog-puppy-young-dog-cute-small-dog-2467149/

Counselling (2017 February 23). *Dog puppy Jack Russell Chihuahua baby cute.* Pixabay. [Image] https://pixabay.com/photos/dog-puppy-jack-russell-chihuahua-2091849/

Gouley, Laurie. (2016, February 28). *Brown and white short coat medium size dog.* Pexels . [Image]. https://

www.pexels.com/photo/brown-and-white-short-coat-medium-size-dog-53261/

Henry, Matthew. (n.d.). *Frozen moment capturing the bark of a white and black sled dog.* Burst. [Image]. https://burst.shopify.com/photos/frozen-moment-capturing-the-bark-of-a-white-and-black-sled-dog?q=dog+bark

Lim, Hannah. (2018 June 20). *Pink wall full of dogs.* Unsplash. [Image]. https://unsplash.com/photos/U6nlG0Y5sfs

Murdoch, Scott. (n.d.) Mini doberman pinscher face. Burst. [Image]. https://burst.shopify.com/photos/mini-doberman-pinscher-face?q=dog

RoAll. (2019 August 17). *Handshake welcome gesture dog human shaking hands.* Pixabay. [Image]. https://pixabay.com/photos/handshake-welcome-gesture-dog-4411471/

VIVIAN6276. (2018 August 10). *Dog hunting dog dressage obedience learning.* Pixabay. [Image]. https://pixabay.com/photos/dog-hunting-dog-dressage-obedience-3594050/

Woodsilver (2017 March 10). *dog-agility-training-jumping-breed.* Pixabay. [Image]. https://pixabay.

com/photos/dog-agility-training-jumping-breed-2126678/